# Preface

The purpose of this translation of Collado's *Ars Grammaticae Iaponicae Linguae* of 1632 is to make more readily available to the scholarly community an annotated version of this significant document in the history of both Japanese language study and grammatical description in general.

Collado's work, derived in all its significant features from the *Arte da lingoa de Iapam* completed in 1608 by João Rodriguez, is in a strict, scholarly sense less valuable than its precursor. However, if used with the *Arte* as a simplified restatement of the basic structure of the language, Collado's Grammar offers to the student of the Japanese language an invaluable ancillary tool for the study of the colloquial language of the early 17th Century.

While less extensive and less carefully edited than the *Arte*, Collado's Grammar has much to recommend it as a document in the history of grammatical description. It is an orthodox description attempting to fit simple Japanese sentences into the framework established for Latin by the great Spanish humanist Antonio Lebrija. Thus, as an application of pre-Cartecian grammatical theory to the structure of a non-Indo-European language, the *Ars Grammaticae* is an important document worthy of careful examination by those wishing insight into the origins of what three centuries later was to become the purview of descriptive linguistics.

The present translation was begun with the able assistance of Ms. Roberta Galli whose contribution to my understanding of the Latin text is most gratefully acknowledged. For his continued encouragement in this undertaking I am grateful to Professor Roy Andrew Miller. Thanks are also due to the Graduate School of the University of Kansas for its support in the preparation of the manuscript and to Ms. Sue Schumock whose capable typing turned a scribbled, multi-lingual draft into a legible manuscript. The imperfections are my own.

R.L.S.

Lawrence, Kansas
May, 1975

---

## Introduction

In 1632, as the Christian Century in Japan was drawing swiftly to a close, three works pertaining to the Japanese language were being published at Rome by the Congregation for the Propagation of the Faith. These works were by the Spanish Dominican Father, Diego Collado (d. 1638), who had spent the years from 1619 to 1622 in Japan. Their publication clearly reflects the vitality of the missionary spirit in that age as well as the important place reserved for language study in the propagation of the faith.

The first two works, whose manuscripts had been prepared in Madrid the year before, were a grammar and a dictionary of Japanese. The third, prepared in 1631, while the larger works were being seen through the press, was a guide to the taking of confession written in both Latin and Japanese.[1] The grammar, drafted in Spanish, was published in Latin in 1632 under the title *Ars Grammaticae Iaponicae Linguae*. It is this work that is translated here. The dictionary, only at the last moment supplied with Latin glosses to supplement those in Spanish, was published in the same year with the title *Dictionarium sive Thesauri Linguae Iaponicae Compendium*.[2] Taken together these three works by Collado constitute the final extant efforts of those who studied the Japanese language first hand during the Christian Century.[3]

Two other grammatical works must be mentioned here as central to the proper assessment of Collado's Grammar. They are both by the great Jesuit scholar, Father João Rodnguez (1561-1634);[4] the *Arte da Lingoa de Iapam* (Nagasaki, 1604-8, hereafter the *Arte*), and the *Arte Breve da Lingoa Iapoa* (Macao, 1620, hereafter *Arte Breve*). The first is by any standards the greatest grammatical study of Japanese made during the Christian Century. It is further, as we shall see, the primary source for Collado's Grammar. The *Arte Breve*, on the other hand, is not directly related to Collado's work. Indeed it is clear that Rodriguez' 1620 Macao publication was unknown to Collado. Nevertheless, since the *Arte Breve* is an abbreviated version of the *Arte* with a purpose similar to the *Ars Grammaticae*, a comparison of these two books with respect to the way they systematize the material from the *Arte* is included in this introduction to contribute some insight into the treatment of the Japanese language at the beginning of the Tokugawa Period.

In presenting this translation two potential audiences are envisioned. The first, and more restricted, group is that having an interest in the history of the Japanese language. It is hoped that an English version of this work will make more readily available this significant material pertaining to the Japanese language as spoken in the early modern period. I use the word significant here to avoid granting excessive value to a work which derives such a large portion of its material and insight from Rodriguez' *Arte*.

The second, and wider group for whom this translation is intended is that which has a need for an edited edition of an important document in the history of grammatical description. In this area of scholarship Collado's work is of more than moderate significance. It was accepted for publication by the prestigious Propaganda Press; and, even if those more familiar with Japanese than the editorial board of that Press might have had serious reservations concerning the linguistic accuracy of the text, it is reasonable to assume that the Press judged it to be a good example of grammatical description. It thus represents a grammar of a non-European language which suited the requirements of the day for publication at Rome.[5]

In order to permit this translation of the *Ars Grammaticae* to be of use in both these areas of scholarship I have made an effort to reduce to a minimum those places where a knowledge of either Japanese or Latin is required for the comprehension of the translation. It is sincerely hoped that the result is not an effort that is satisfying to neither, and thus to no one.

Because of the derivative nature of the text, this translation has put aside a number of important philological problems as better dealt with within the context of Rodriguez' grammars. This decision has its most obvious consequences in the section on the arithmetic, where innumerable data require exposition. However, since a basic purpose of this translation is within the context of the history of descriptive grammar, these tantalizing side roads have been left unexplored. It is, nevertheless, hoped that this translation will serve as a convenient tool for those wishing to make a more detailed investigation into the philological questions raised by the text. But I must caution those who would undertake such an inquiry that they had best begin with a careful study of the works of Father Rodriguez.

With its limitations acknowledged, the *Ars Grammaticae Iaponicae Linguae* remains a document worthy of our interest, and I offer this translation in order that Collado's work may more easily find its proper place in the history of descriptive grammar.

## *The Grammatical Framework*

Collado perceived his task to be the presentation of a grammar of Japanese which would have sufficient scope to equip those dedicated to the propagation of the faith with a knowledge of the proper spoken language of his time. While he concludes his grammar with a brief, and rather presumptuous, statement concerning the written language, his purpose is clearly to train his students in the fundamentals of colloquial speech. His sensitivity to this point is demonstrated by his carefully transforming those examples presented by Rodriguez in the written language in the *Arte* into correct colloquial expressions in his own grammar.

The description is, of course, prescriptive. But given its age and its purpose this ought not to be construed in the contemporary, pejorative sense. Collado, as Rodriguez and indeed all the grammarians of the period, felt obligated to train their students in those patterns of speech which were appropriate to the most polite elements of society. Particularly as they addressed themselves to missionaries, they wished to warn them away from such illiteracies as might undermine their capacities to propagate the faith.

The description further reflects the traditional process conceptualization of language. This is particularly obvious in the treatment of the verb. Thus:

> *Praesens subiunctiui fit ex praesenti indicatiui mutato* u *in quo finitur in* eba.... (The present subjunctive is formed from the present indicative by changing the *u* in which it ends to *eba*....) [p. 23].

In general each of the verbal forms is conceived to be the result of a specified alteration of a basic form. Likewise the nouns are treated within the framework of the declension of cases.

The treatment of Japanese forms is based upon a semantic framework within which the formal characteristics of the language are organized. For example, given the construction *aguru coto aró* (p. 31) and its gloss '*Erit hoc quod ist offere: idest offeret* (It will be that he is to offer, or he will offer),' it is clear that the *aguru coto* is classified as an infinitive because of its semantic equivalence to *offere*. The same is true of the latter supine. If the form in Latin is closely associated with such constructions as 'easy to,' or 'difficult to,' the semantically similar form which appears as the element *iomi* in *iominicui* 'difficult to read,' must be classed as the latter supine. Rodriguez in his *Arte Breve* of 1620—unknown to Collado—makes an attempt to classify the structural units of Japanese along more formal lines; but in Collado's treatment the semantic, and for him logical and true, classes established by the formal structure of Latin constitute the theoretical framework through which the Japanese language is to be described.

Collado makes reference to two specific sources of influence upon his grammar. The first is included in the title to the first section of the grammar, Antonius Nebrissensis. It is to this great Spanish humanist, better known as Antonio Lebrija (1444-1522), that Collado turns for the model of his description.

An examination of Lebrija's grammar, the *Introductiones Latinae* (Salamanca, 1481), shows that from the basic outline of his presentation, to the organization of subsections and the selection of terminology, there is little departure by Collado from his predecessor.

Even in such stylistic devices as introducing the interrogatives by giving the form, following it with "to which one responds," and then listing a number of characteristic answers; Collado is faithful to the *Introductiones*.

But it is from his Jesuit colleague, Father João Rodriguez, that Collado receives his most significant influence. There is no section of his grammar that does not reflect Rodriguez' interpretation of the raw linguistic data of Japanese. On the basis of the innumerable examples taken from Rodriguez—most of the substantive sentences are directly quoted from the *Arte*—as well as the parallel listing of forms and identical descriptions of certain grammatical phenomena, it is clear that the writing of the *Ars Grammaticae Iaponicae Linguae* consisted to no small degree of abridging the exhaustive material contained in Rodriguez' grammar and arranging it within the framework of Lebrija's *Introductiones*.

To say that Collado followed Lebrija in the general structure of his description is not to imply that he fell heir to all of his precursor's virtues. The Salamanca grammar of 1481 is a masterpiece of orderly presentation. Printed in *lettera formata* with carefully indented subdivisions, it offers the student a clear display of the conjugational system as well as long columns of Latin examples of a given grammatical structure, accompanied on the right side of the page with Spanish equivalents. Collado makes little effort at copying this orderly display. There are in his presentation no paradigms, but instead only loosely connected sentences that talk the student through the various forms of the conjugation; and there is no orderly array of examples. Add to this the innumerable factual and typographical errors, and one is left with a presentation that lacks most of the basic scholarly virtues of its precursor.

A similar criticism may be leveled against the work from the point of view of Rodriguez' influence. Without matching the *Introductiones* in orderliness, the *Arte* more than compensates for its casual format by containing a mass of exhaustively collected and scrupulously presented linguistic data.[6] There was available no better source than the *Arte* from which Collado might have culled his examples of Japanese.

One doubt that remains in assessing Collado's use of Rodriguez' material is that perhaps his presentation of the most readily understandable material in the *Arte* is not so much an effort on his part to simplify the learning of Japanese for his students, as it is a reflection of his lack of adequate familiarity with the language he was teaching.

## *The Phonological System*

A study of the phonological data reveals the *Ars Grammaticae Iaponicae Linguae* to be of minimal historical value. Any student of the phonology of early modern Japanese should turn to the far more reliable work of Father Rodriguez. Nevertheless, certain aspects of Collado's transcription require our attention.

The most obvious innovation in the representation of the language is Collado's transcription with an *i* of the palatal consonant which all his contemporaries record with a *y*. Thus in the text we find *iomi* and *coie* (terms for native words and Chinese borrowings) where Rodriguez writes *yomi* and *coye*. This change was affected while the text was being translated from the Spanish manuscript which uses *y*; and Collado himself must have felt the innovation to be of dubious value since he retained *y* for the spellings in the *Dictionarium*.[7]

Collado's handling of the nasal sounds is too inconsistent to be a reliable source for phonological data. Given his rather awkward specification that nasalization is predictable before what we must assume he means to be the voiced stops and affricates,[8] his grammar presents an uncomfortably irregular pattern in the transcription of the phenomena. Thus, on page 39 we find *vo mõdori aró ca?* as well as *modori aró ca?*. Again, what he presents as the ending *zũba* in his description of the formation of the negative conditional (p. 34) appears in *tovazunba* in its only occurrence in a sample sentence (p. 62). To further confound the issue such forms as *tovazunba* and *qinpen* occur in contrast to *sambiacu, varambe*, and *varãbe*.

In Chart 1 the traditional pattern of the *gojūonzu* (chart of 50 sounds) is followed as a convenient framework in which to display the transcriptional system employed by Collado.

### Chart1

## COLLADO'STRANSCRIPTIONSYSTEM

*The Simple Series*

| | /#/ | /k/ | /g/ | /s/ | /z/ | /t/ | /d/ | /n/ | /φ/ | /b/ | /p/ | /m/ | /y/ | /r/ | /w/ |
|---|---|---|---|---|---|---|---|---|---|---|---|---|---|---|---|
| /a/ | a | ca | ga | sa | za | ta | da | na | fa | ba | pa | ma | ia | ra | va |
| /i/ | i | qi | gui | xi | ji | chi | gi | ni | fi | bi | pi | mi | - | ri | - |
| /u/ | u | cu | gu | su | zu | tçu | zzu | nu | fu | bu | pu | mu | iu | ru | - |
| /e/ | [ie] | qe | gue | xe | je | te | de | ne | fe | be | pe | me | ie | re | - |
| /o/ | [vo] | co | go | so | zo | to | do | no | fo | bo | po | mo | io | ro | vo |
| *The Long Series* | | | | | | | | | | | | | | | |
| /au/ | [vó] | có | gó | só | zó | tó | dó | nó | fó | bó | (pó) | mó | ió | ró | vó |
| /uu/ | ú | cú | (gú) | (sú) | - | (tçú) | - | - | fú | (bú) | (pú) | - | iú | rú | - |

/ou/ [vô] cô (gô) sô zô tô dô nô (fô) (bô) pô mô iô rô vô

*The Palatal and Labial Series*

| | /ky/ | /gy/ | /sy/ | /zy/ | /ty/ | /dy/ | /ny/ | /φy/ | /by/ | /py/ | /my/ | /ry/ | /kw/ | /gw/ |
|---|---|---|---|---|---|---|---|---|---|---|---|---|---|---|
| /a/ | (qua) | (guia) | xa | ja | cha | gia | (nha) | fia | bia | pia | (mia) | (ria) | qua | gua |
| /u/ | qui | (guiu) | xu | ju | (chu) | (giu) | (nhu) | (fiu) | - | - | (miu) | (riu) | - | - |
| /o/ | qio | guio | xo | (jo) | cho | gio | (nho) | (fio) | (bio) | - | (mio) | (rio) | - | - |
| /au/ | qió | guió | xó | jó | chó | gió | - | (fió) | (bió) | - | mió | (rió) | quó | guó |
| /uu/ | (qiú) | (guiú) | (xú) | jú | (chú) | giú | nhú | - | - | - | - | (riú) | - | - |
| /ou/ | qiô | (guiô) | xô | jô | chô | giô | nhô | fiô | (biô) | piô | (miô) | (riô) | - | - |
| | | gueô | | | | geô | neô | | beô | | | reô | | |

In this chart the phonemic grid is presented in a broad phonetic notation while the underlined entries are in the form used by the text. Dashes indicate sequences which do not occur in the Christian material; while the forms in parentheses are sequences which do not occur in the text but have been reconstructed on the basis of the overall system from sequences attested to elsewhere. The forms *ie, vo, vó,* and *vô* have been placed in brackets to indicate that neither /e/, /o/, /oo/, or /au/ occur in the syllable initial position; and, where in the modern language they do, the text regularly spells that with an initial *i* or *v*. The forms in *eô* at the foot of the chart represent sequences that are phonetically identical to the forms above them, but which are transcribed differently to reflect morphological considerations; e.g., the form *agueô* from the stem *ague*. The phonetic values of /au/, /uu/, and /ou/ are [ɔ:], [u:], and [o:].

Two aspects of the usage of *q* should be noticed. First, as in the *Arte*, *c* is changed to *q* before *o* and *u*, when the sequence occurs at a morphological juncture; e.g., *ioqu* 'well,' and *iqó* 'I shall go.' (This rule does not extend to *a* in such contexts; cf., *iocatta* 'was good.') Second, in contrast to the system used by Rodriguez, Collado does not feel compelled to follow *q* with *u* in all contexts. Thus what Rodriguez spells as *queredomo* Collado spells as *qeredomo*. Finally, the text records one usage of the letter *h* in the exclamation *ha*.

## *The Morphological System*

Collado's treatment of the morphology contains one quite obvious difference from those of his predecessors: he isolates the particles of the language as separate elements of the structure. While his effort is more or less carelessly maintained by the type setter, his attempt to establish a division between the semantemes (*shi*) and the morphemes (*ji*) of Japanese by establishing formal distance between his *verba* and *particula*, reflects his consciousness that the morphological elements in Japanese are of a different order than those in Latin. At times, such as when he describes the preterit subjunctive as *agueta raba*, his divisions fly in the face of derivational history. But he can claim a reasonable justification for his decision by citing Rodriguez' rule for the formation of this form; "add *raba* to the preterit of the verb" (*Arte*, 18v). Perhaps it is a prejudice founded upon familiarity with contemporary romanizations, but I cannot help but consider this attempt to give greater independence to the particles as an improvement in the representation of the morphological system.

In all other significant facets of the morphology Collado follows the principles established by Rodriguez with the one exception that in the over-all systematization of the verbal formation and conjugation he follows the classifications established in Lebrija's *Introductiones* rather than those which Rodriguez inherited from the *Institutiones* of Alverez. The most significant difference between the two systems is the use by Lebrija of the term subjunctive in his description of the moods where Rodriguez gives independent status to the conjunctive, conditional, concessive, and potential. As we shall see, after presenting the conjugational system of the verb within the framework of Lebrija, Collado breaks the expected sequence of his description of the verb to interject a section on conditional constructions and another on those of the potential.

In the treatment of the tenses Collado breaks with Rodriguez in not attempting to establish an imperfect for Japanese, but he does follow him in the overall classification of the conjugations. Thus:[9]

| | | |
|---|---|---|
| 1st Conjugation | verbs ending in *e*, *gi*, and *ji* (*xi* and *maraxi*) | e.g., *ague*, *uru* |
| 2nd Conjugation | verbs ending in *i* | e.g., *iomi*, *u* |
| 3rd Conjugation | verbs ending in *ai*, *oi*, and *ui* | e.g., *narai*, *ó* |

To the description of this general system Collado adds the treatment of the substantive verbs. This section in many respects is the weakest in his grammar with a portion of his description lost in composing the final text.

Since Collado does not, as Rodriguez, present the conjugations in paradigmatic form, I have extracted from his presentation the most representative forms of the verb *ague, uru* for each of the categories of the system, and presented them in Chart 2 for reference.

## CHART2

## THECONJUGA TIONALSYSTEM

| | *Affirmative* | *Negative* |
|---|---|---|
| | INDICATIVE MOOD | |
| Present | aguru | aguenu |
| Perfect | agueta | aguenanda |
| Pluperfect | aguete atta | aguenande atta |
| Future | agueôzu | aguru mai |
| Future perfect | aguete arŏzu | —— |
| | IMPERATIVE MOOD | |
| Present | ague io | aguru na |
| Future | agueôzu | aguru mai |
| | OPTATIVE MOOD | |
| Present | avare ague io caxi | avare aguru na caxi |
| Preterit | agueôzu mono vo | aguru mai mono vo |
| Future | avare ague io caxi | avare aguru na caxi |
| | SUBJUNCTIVE MOOD | |
| Present | agureba | agueneba |
| Perfect | agueta reba | aguenanda reba |
| Pluperfect | aguete atta reba | —— |
| Future | agueô toqi | aguru mai qereba |
| | PERMISSIVE SUBJUNCTIVE MOOD | |
| Present | agueredomo | aguenedomo |

| | | |
|---|---|---|
| Preterit | agueta redomo | aguenanda redomo |
| Future | agueôzu redomo | aguru mai qeredomo |
| | INFINITIVE | |
| Present | aguru coto | aguenu coto |
| Preterit | agueta coto | aguenanda coto |
| Future | agueô coto | aguru mai coto |
| | GERUND IN *DI* | |
| Present | aguru [jibun] | aguenu [jibun] |
| Future | agueô [jibun] | aguru mai [jibun] |
| | GERUND IN *DO* | |
| —— | aguete | agueĩde |
| | GERUND IN *DUM* | |
| Present | aguru tame | aguenu tame |
| Future | agueô tame | aguru mai tame |
| | SUPINE IN *TUM* | |
| —— | ague ni | —— |
| | SUPINE IN *TU* | |
| —— | ague | —— |
| | PARTICIPLE | |
| Present | aguru fito | aguenu fito |
| Preterit | agueta fito | aguenando fito |
| Future | agueô fito | aguru mai fito |

The forms treated separately are:

THE CONDITIONAL

| | | |
|---|---|---|
| Present | agueba | aguezũba |
| Preterit | agueta raba | aguenanda raba |
| Future | agueô naraba | aguru mai naraba |
| | THE POTENTIAL | |
| Present | aguru ró | aguenu coto mo arózu |
| Preterit | aguetçu ró | aguenanzzu ró |
| Future | agueôzu ró | aguru mai coto mo arózu |

### *The Structure of Collado's and Rodriguez' Descriptions Contrasted*

In every section of his description, Collado is indebted to the material presented by Rodriguez in his *Arte da Lingoa de Iapam*. The structure of the *Ars Grammaticae*, however, follows a much more simplistic design than that of the *Arte*. As a consequence Collado found it necessary to assemble his data from various sections of Rodriguez' description. In the paragraphs which follow we will briefly sketch the structural relation between these two grammars.

As he clearly states in his title to the main portion of the grammar Collado bases his description on the *Introductiones* of Antonio Lebriya, and more specifically upon that portion of the great Latin grammar which dealt with the parts of speech. Further, he limits himself to the spoken language rather than attempting, as does Rodriguez, an integrated treatment of both the spoken and written grammars.

Under these influences Collado's grammar takes on the following form:

A Prologue (including the phonology) ... 3-5
The Body of the Grammar (by parts of speech) ... 6-61
A Brief Syntax ... 61-66
A Treatment of the Arithmetic ... 66-74
A Note on the Written Language ... 74-75

In contrast Rodriguez' *Arte*, prepared under the influence of Alvarez' *Institutiones*, develops its description over the span of three books which treat both the spoken and written grammar in progressively greater detail. Thus:

The Introduction ... iii-v

Book I

The Declensions ... 1-2v
The Conjugations ... 2v-54
The Parts of Speech (*Rudimenta*) ... 55-80v

Book II

The Syntax of the Parts of Speech ... 83-168
Styles, Pronunciation, Poetics, etc. ... 168-184

Book III

The Written Language ... 184v-206v
Names, Titles, etc. ... 206v-212v
The Arithmetic ... 212v-239

Given these differing formats[10] it is clear that Collado is unable to cope adequately with the more complex aspects of the grammar, specifically those syntactic constructions to which Rodriguez devotes almost an entire book.

An analysis of Collado's description and a listing of the portions of Rodriguez' grammar from which material was taken yields the following:

| *Collado* | *Rodriguez* |
|---|---|
| Phonology (3-5) | Parts of Speech (55-58)<br>Book III (173-179v) |
| Nouns (6-13) | Declensions (1-2v)<br>Parts of Speech (59-61) |
| Adjectives (9-11, 32-33) | Declensions (2-2v)<br>Conjugations (47-52)<br>Parts of Speech (61-67) |
| Pronouns (13-18) | Declensions (2v)<br>Parts of Speech (67-68) |
| Verbs (18-49) | Conjugations (6v-54v)<br>Parts of Speech (69-73)<br>Syntax (83v-112v) |
| Adverbs (49-57) | Parts of Speech (73v-77)<br>Syntax (113-125) |
| Prepositions (57-59) | Parts of Speech (73-73v)<br>Syntax (140-148v) |
| Conjunctions (59-60) | Parts of Speech (76-76v)<br>Syntax (130-137) |
| Exclamations (60-61) | Parts of Speech (76-76v) |

| | |
|---|---|
| | { Syntax (125-130) |
| Syntax (61-66) | Book II (83-168) |
| Arithmetic (66-75) | Book III (212v-239) |
| Written Language (74-75) | Book III (184v-206v) |

Two aspects of Japanese were not able to be described with any degree of satisfaction by Collado; the adjectives (*adjectiva*) and the prepositions (*praepositio*). His difficulties, attributable to the basic structural difference between Latin and Japanese, were compounded by the fact that Rodriguez too was unable to find a satisfactory solution to their description.

With respect to the adjectives, Collado attempts to deal with their functions in the manner appropriate to Latin, that is as a sub-class of nouns (pp. 9-11). He also recognizes their formal similarity to the verb and treats them briefly as a sub-class of the substantive verb (pp. 32-33), but his heavy reliance upon the semantic categories of Latin does not permit him to follow Rodriguez who is able more clearly to recognize their formal as well as their functional distinctiveness.

Concerning prepositions, Collado was confronted with an all but insurmountable taxonomic problem. Here too Rodriguez was unable to develop a completely satisfactory descriptive framework. In the *Arte* the term *posposição* is used for those particles which function in a manner similar to the Latin prepositions; e.g., *tameni, taixite,* and *tomoni* (cf. 73-73v and 140-148v); the term *artigo* is used for those particles having the functions of the inflectional endings of Latin; e.g., *ga, ye,* and *ni* (cf. 1-2, 78, and 137-140); and the general term *particula* is used to cover the broad spectrum of particles that include adverbs, conjunctions, and exclamations, as well as those otherwise unaccounted for elements which end phrases, clauses, and sentences; e.g., *no, nite,* and *yo* (cf. 77-78 and 144-154v).

Collado, rather than attempting to refine the system suggested by Rodriguez, follows the *Arte* in listing as *praepositio* those elements which translate the Latin prepositions (pp. 57-59) but uses the term *particula* to cover all the other particles of the language.

This tendency of Collado's to retreat from the challenging problems left unresolved by Rodriguez constitutes the greatest weakness of his description. Given concise grammatical descriptions on the one hand and over-simplified versions of previous works on the other, the *Ars Grammaticae Iaponicae Linguae* unfortunately falls among the latter.

In his shorter work, the *Arte Breve* of 1620, Rodriguez retains the same general format, but makes every effort to reduce the description to its barest essentials. Thus:

Book I

A General Note on the Language ... 1-2
An Essay on How to Learn the Language ... 2v-6
The Orthography ... 6-8
Composition of the Syllables ... 8v-9v
The Way to Write and Pronounce the Letters ... 10-12v
The Declension of Nouns ... 13-18
The Conjugation and Formation of Verbs ... 18-52

Book II

The Rudimenta ... 52-59v
The Syntax ... 59v-66v

Book III

The Written Language ... 67-75
The Various Kinds of Names ... 75v-98v

Of particular interest in the context of Collado's grammar is the manner in which Rodriguez displays the verbal system. While the *Ars Grammaticae* presents the verbal system as a series of alterational rules to be applied to the base forms, the *Arte Breve* goes even further than the *Arte* to differentiate the formational rules from the conjugational displays. Rodriguez tries several devices to elucidate his material. For example, Charts A and B below represent very early attempts to use a bordered format for linguistic description.

In order to indicate the differences to be found between the descriptions presented by Rodriguez and Collado, I have extracted the formational rules from the *Arte Breve* and, setting aside only two short appendices dealing with variant forms, present them here in their entirety.

*THE CONJUGATION AND FORMATION OF THE TENSES AND MOODS OF THE VERBS*

*All the verbs of this language may be reduced* (se reduzem) *to four affirmative and three negative conjugations. This is because the negative conjugation of the adjectival verb, which we discussed before,*[11] *agrees with the second of the three conjugations; and the conjugation of the substantive verb* Sŏrai, Sŏrŏ, *or* soro, *which is an abbreviated form of* Samburai, samburŏ[12] *both in the affirmative and the negative is reduced to the third conjugation. At this point we will treat the three affirmative and three negative ordinary conjugations of the regular personal verbs.*[13] *Following this, and on account of its particular usage and formation, we will discuss the conjugation of the adjectival verb.*

*The verbs of this language do not change* (naõ fẽ variedade) *to show person and number as do those of Latin; rather, one form* (voz) *is used for all persons, singular and plural. Number and person are understood according to the subject* (Naminativo [*sic*]), *or pronoun, which is joined to the verb. The moods of the verb, which in this language have distinct forms for the tenses, are indicative, imperative, conjunctive, conditional, and preterit participle. The remaining moods are made up of these forms joined to certain particles. Each mood has but three tenses which have distinct forms; these are preterit, present, and future. These forms are signified by the Japanese terms* (vocabulos) Quaco, ghenzai, mirai. *The preterit imperfect and pluperfect are made up of the present, preterit, and preterit participle together with the substantive verb, as will be seen below in the conjugations.*

*Concerning the formation of the tenses and moods of the verbs in general, one is reminded that to understand the actual root* (raiz) *and the natural formation of all the tenses and moods, both affirmative and negative, it is extremely important to take notice of the usage of the* Goyn,[14] *which are the five vowels* (cinco letras vogaes) *in the syllables which are below each aforementioned formation; and that it is also important to understand* Canadzucai,[15] *which is the way to write with* Firagana *as well as the way one joins together syllables, or letters, to form other words* (palauras), *while noticing which syllable is changed by which, what constitutes long, short, or diphthongal syllables, which combinations cause contraction* (sincope), *which cause augmentation* (incremento) *of the verb, whether one makes a syllable liquid* (liquescit)[16] *or not, and how the tenses of the moods are written with the same* Cana.[17] *The term* Goyn, *not only indicates the syllables, or* Cana, *which are transformed to others, such as* Fa, Fe, Fi, Fo, Fu, *which are changed to the closely related sounds* Ba, Be, Bi, Bo, Bu *and* Pa, Pe, Pi, Po, Pu*; but it also indicates another kind of change from one sound to another in the same order* (ordem), *as happens among the syllables* Fa, Fe, Fi, Fo, Fu. Ba, Be, Bi, Bo, Bu. Ma, Me, Mi, Mo, Mu, *etc. where often by rule* (regna) Ma *is changed to* Mi*; or to the contrary* Bu *to* Ba *and* Bi *to* Ba, *and likewise for others. The greater part of the formation of the tenses of each mood is confined to such changes, as is clearly seen in the way one writes the tense forms with* Cana. *It is to this that another change belongs. That which exists among those syllables having a certain relationship and rapport between them, as* Ma, Fa, Ba, Pa*;* Me, Fe, Be, Pe*;* Mi, Fi, Bi, Pi*;* Mo, Fo, Bo, Po*;* Mu, Fu, Bu, Pu*; with* Mu *and* V. *Thus, what is written* Vma *in* Cana *is written* Muma, *and* Mume *written for* Vme *in order to conform more closely to its pronunciation.*[18] *Also* Mu *is written for* Bu[19] *so that all the harmony* (armonia) *in the formations of this language are contained in the rules for* Goyn *and* Canadzucai. *Those who are informed see, as native speakers, how the tenses are formed for any mood, and which letter, or syllable, must be changed to another to affect a formation. Concerning this matter there is a booklet*[20] *which teaches* Canadzucai, *and the general rules on the subject. Teachers should have this booklet to teach more easily and advantageously those students who are learning* Cana. *Lacking a knowledge of* Goyn *and* Canadzucai, *some of the rules which until now have been used in the formation of verbs (some of which I have let remain as they were), are not the original and natural rules as are the* Goyn.[21] *They are rather devices, some forming affirmative tenses and moods from negative forms and others forming them from yet other more remote sources, which appear to correspond to formational rules, but for which the proper rules are not known. The fact is that the affirmative as well as negative are formed from the affirmative, beginning with the root, as will be seen below.*

*Speaking in general of the formation of the verb, the forms of the indicative and imperative moods of all three conjugations are formed from the root of the verb. The rest of the tenses in the other affirmative moods are formed from either the indicative or imperative forms. In the same way, the negative indicative present is formed from the root of the verb and the other tenses of the indicative are formed from the present form. The other negative moods are formed from the indicative forms.*

### Formation of the Tenses for the Indicative and Imperative Moods of the Verbs of the First Affirmative Conjugation

*The final syllables of the roots of the first affirmative conjugation, by which the verbs conjugated here are known, and from which the tenses of the indicative will be formed, end in* E, *with the exception of the verb "to do,"* Xi, *or* Ii, *with its compounds and certain other verbs which end in* I. *The verbs which belong to the first conjugation, are as follows* [*in Charts A & B*].

*The verb* Xi *"to do," with its compounds ending in* Xi *or* Ii, *follows the formation of the verbs of the first conjugation.* Ii *is* Xi *which has been changed* (alterado) *to* Ii *because it follows the letter* N. Xi *conforms to the rules for the syllables which are changed* (se mudam) *to others. Thus:*

| | | |
|---|---|---|
| Xi | *In the present change* Xi *to* Suru. *In the preterit add* Ta *to the root. In the future change* Xi *to* Xeô. *In the imperative change* Xi *to* Xe *and add* Yo, i, *or* sai. *In the negative add* Nu, *or* zu *to* Xe. | Suru, xita, xeô, ôzu, ôzuru, xeyo, xenu, *or* zu. |
| Faixi | | Faisuru, faixita, faixeô, faixeyo, faixenu. |
| Tayxi[22] | | Tassuru, taxxita, taxxeô, taxxeyo, taxxenu. |
| Gaxxi | | Gassuru, gaxxita, gaxxeô, gaxxeyo, gaxxenu. |
| Zonji | *In the present* Ii *is changed to* Zuru. *In the preterit* Ta *is added to the root. In the future* Ii *is changed to* Ieô, *etc.* | Zonzuru, zonjita, zonjeô, ôzu, ôzuru, zonjeyo, zonjenu. |
| Caronji | | Caronzuru, caronjita,*etc.* |
| Vomonji | | Vomonzuru, vomonjita. |
| Sanji | | Sanzuru, sanjita. |
| Goranji | | Goranzuru, goranjita. |
| Soranji | | Soranzuru, soranjita. |
| Ganji | | Canzuru, canjita. |
| Manji | | Manzuru, manjita. |

*Many of these verbs have another, less used, form made by adding* Ru *to the root; e.g.,* Abi, abiru; Mochiy, mochiyru; xiy, xiyru. *Among these are some that have only this second form and lack the first; e.g.,* Mi, miru; Ni, niru; Fi, firu; Cagammi, cagammiru; Ki, kiru *"to dress," as distinct from* Ki, kuru *"to come"; and* y, yru.

### Chart A

[The Formation of First Conjugation Verbs Ending in *E*]

| *Syllables* | *Roots* | *Formation* | *Present* | *Preterit* | *Future* | *Imperative* | *Negative* |
|---|---|---|---|---|---|---|---|
| Te, | Tate, | *In the present change* Te *to* Tçuru. *The remainder are from the root. See above.* | Tatçuru. | Tateta. | Tateô, ôzu, ôzuru. | Tateyo. Tatei, tatesay.[23] | Tatenu, *or*, zu. |
| | Fate, | | Fatçuru. | Fateta. | Fateô, ôzu, ôzuru. | Fateyo, *etc.* | Fatenu, *or*, zu. |

| Ie, | Maje, | *Change* Ie *to* Zuru *in the present. The remainder are from the root. See above.* | Mazuru. | Majeta. | Majeô. | Majeyo, *etc.* | Majenu, *or*, zu. |
|---|---|---|---|---|---|---|---|
| Xe, | Saxe, | *In the present change* Xe *to* Suru. *The remainder are from the root. See above.* | Sasuru. | Saxeta. | Saxeô. | Saxeyo. | Saxenu, *or*, zu. |
| | Mairaxe, | | Mairasuru. | Mairaxeta. | Mairaxeô. | Mairaxeyo, *etc.* | Mairaxenu, *or*, zu. |

Chart B

| *Syllables* | *Roots* | *Formation* | *Present* | *Preterit* | *Future* | *Imperative* | *Negative* |
|---|---|---|---|---|---|---|---|
| Be, | Curabe, | *In the present tense of these eight forms, change* E *to* Vru. *In the preterit add* Ta *to the root. In the future* ô, ôzu, ôzuru *to the root. In the Negative present add* Nu, *or* zu *to the root.* | Curaburu. | Curabeta. | Curabeô, ôzu, ôzuru. | Curabeyo, ei, sai. | Curabenu, *or*, Curabezu. |
| Fe, | Fe, | | Furu, *or*, feru. | Feta. | Feô, ôzu, ôzuru. | Feyo, fei, fesai. | fenu, fezu. |
| Ghe, | Aghe, | | Aghuru. | Agheta. | Agheô, | Agheyo, *etc.* | Aghenu, *etc.* |
| Ke, | Tokoke, | | Todokuru. | Todoketa. | Todokeô. *etc.* | Todokenu, *etc.* | |
| Me, | Motome, | | Motomuru. | Motometa. | Motomeô. | Motomeyo, *etc.* | Motomenu, *etc.* |
| Ne, | Fane, | | Fanuru. | Faneta. | Faneô. | Faneyo. | Fanenu. |
| Re, | Fanare, | | Fanaruru. | Fanareta. | Fanareô. | Fanareyo. | Fanarenu. |
| Ye, | Ataye, | | Atayuru. | Atayeta. | Atayeô. | Atayeyo. | Atayenu. |
| [De,] | De, | *In the present change* De *to* | Dzuru. | Deta. | Deô, ôzu, *etc.* | Deyo, *etc.* | Denu. |

| | Ide, | Dzuru. | Idzuru. | Ideta. | Ideô, ôzu. | Ideyo. | Idenu. |
|---|---|---|---|---|---|---|---|
| | Mŏde, | *The other tenses are formed, as above, from the root.* | Mŏdzuru. | Mŏdeta. | *This verb is defective and lacks other forms.* | | |
| | Mede, | | Medzuru. | Medeta. | *This verb is defective and has no other forms.* | | |

### Formation of the Optative, Conjunctive, and Conditional Moods, and the Participle

*The optative mood does not have forms of its own but compensates for this in part by adding to the imperative certain particles which indicate desire, in part by adding to the future indicative particles which show regret for not doing something, and in part by circumlocutions with the conditional mood and certain particles, as will be seen in the conjugations.*

*The conjunctive mood has two sorts of proper forms. The first is the common and ordinary form ending in* Eba, *corresponding to the Latin* cum. *The other ends in* Domo, *corresponding to the particle "although* (posto que)." *The other verbs of this mood do not have their own forms, but are expressed by circumlocutions as we shall see.*[24]

*The present tense of the first conjunctive is formed from the present indicative by changing the final* Ru *to* Reba; *e.g.,* Motomureba. *For the preterit* Reba *is added to the preterit indicative; e.g.,* Motometareba. *For the future the final* Ru *of the third form of the future indicative is changed to* Reba; *e.g.,* Motomeôzureba. *For a second form of the future the syllable* Rŏ *is added to the indicative preterit perfect; e.g.,* Motometarŏ. *This particle is* Ran *in the written language; e.g.,* Motometaran.[25] *An utterance* (oraçam) *does not end in this form, but must be followed by a noun.*[26]

*The present tense of the second conjunctive is formed by changing the final* Ru *of the present indicative to* Redomo; *e.g.,* Motomuredomo. *For the preterit* Redomo *is added to the indicative preterit perfect; e.g.,* Motometaredomo. *Strictly speaking this form is* Motomete aredomo, *losing the* E *of the participle. Furthermore,* Motometa, *together with the other preterit forms in* Ta *is from* Motometearu *which is first elided to* Motometaru *and then by common usage* (pratica) *to* Motometa. *All of which is seen in its* Canadzucai. *For the future, the final* Ru *of the future indicative is changed to* Redomo; *e.g.,* Motomeôzuredomo.

*The conditional mood, for the present tense, is formed by adding the syllable* Ba *to the root of the verb and* Naraba *or* Ni voiteua *to the present tense form; e.g.,* Motomeba, motomuru naraba, *and* motomuruni voiteua. *For the preterit,* Raba, Naraba, *or* Ni voiteua *are added to the indicative preterit; e.g.,* Motometaraba, *which is in reality* Motomete araba, motometa naraba, *and* motometani voiteua. *For the future* Naraba *or* Ni voiteua *are added to the future forms; e.g.,* Motomeô naraba *and* motomeôni voiteua. *The present tense forms are also used for the future.*

### Verbs of the First Conjugation That End in *I*

*There are some irregular verbs ending in* I *which follow the formational rules of the first conjugation, both affirmative and negative. There are a precise number of them. Those which have been found to date are shown below. They are formed for the present indicative by changing* I *to* Uru, *for the preterit by adding* Ta *to the root of the verb, and for the future by adding long* û, ûzu, *or* ûzuru *to the same root. For the present conditional* Ba *is added to the root, for the preterit* Raba *is added to the preterit indicative, and for the future* Naraba *is added to the future indicative. For the present conjunctive the* Ru *of the present indicative is changed to* Reba, *for the preterit* Reba *is added to the same preterit indicative, and for the future the final* Ru *of the future is changed to* Reba. *All the other forms are formed as has been stated for the formation of the first conjugation. Thus:*[27]

Abi {
Abi, aburu, abita, abiû, ûzu, ûzuru, abiyo, *or* sai, abiba, taraba.
Cabi, caburu, cabita, cabiû, ûzu, ûzuru, biyo, sai, biba, bitaraba.
Carabi, caraburu, bita, biû, ûzu, ûzuru, biyo, sai, biba, taraba
Sabi, saburu, sabita, sabiû, ûzu, ûzuru, sabiyo, bisai, biba, taraba
Vabi, vaburu, vabita, vabiû, ûzu, ûzuru, yo, sai, biba, bitaraaba.

| | |
|---|---|
| Obi | Nobi, buru, bita, biû, ûzu, ûzuru, biyo, bisai, biba, bitaraba. |
| | Corobi, buru, bita, biû, biûzu, ûzuru, biyo, bisai, biba, bitaraba. |
| | Forobi, buru, bita, biû, ûzu, ûzuru, biyo, bisai, biba, bitaraba. |
| | Fitobi, bu, bita, biû, ûzu, ûzuru, biyo, bisai, biba, bitaraba. |
| | Fokorobi, bu, bita, biû, ûzu, ûzuru, biyo, bisai, biba, bitaraba. |
| Ubi | Furubi, bu, bita, biû, ûzu, ûzuru, biyo, bisai, biba, bitaraba. |

| | | |
|---|---|---|
| Vochi, | Chi *to* Tçuru | Votçuru, chita, chiû, chiyo, chiba, tçureba. |
| Cuchi, | | Cutçuru, chita, chiû, chiyo, chiba, tçureba. |
| Fagi, | *Change* Gi *to* Dzu | Fadzuru, fagita, giû, giyo, giba, gitaraba. |
| Vogi, | | Vodzuru, gita, giû, giyo, giba, gitaraba. |
| Negi, | | Nedzuru, gita, giû, giyo, giba, gitaraba. |
| Mochiy | *the final* Y *to* Yuru | Mochiyuru, mochiyta, chiyû, yûzu, ûzuru, iyo, yba, yttaraba. |
| Xiy, | | Xiyuru, xiyta, yû iyo, yba ytaraba. |
| Mimixiy, | | Mimixiyta, mimixiyte, *Defective*. |
| Mexiy, | | Mexiytaru, mexiyte, *Defective*. |

Y, yru, yta, yû, ûzu, ûzuru, yyo, yba, yreba. *To be*
Ki, kiru, kita kiû, kiyo, *&c. To wear*
Ki, kuru, kita, kô, kôzu, kôzuru, koyo *or* koi. *To Come*
Coru, coruru, corita, coriû, *&c.*
Furi, fururu, furita, furiû, *&c.*
Iki, ikuru, ikita, ikiû, *&c.*
Ideki, idekuru, idekita, idekiû, *&c.*
Deki, dekuru, dekita, dekiû, *&c.*
Voki, vokuru, vokita, vokiû, *&c.*
Tçuki, tçukuru, tçukita, tçukiû, *&c.*
Vori, voruru, vorita, voriû, *&c.*
Vrami, vramuru, vramita, vramiû, *&c.*
Cagammi, cagammiru, cagammita, cagammiû, *&c.*
Mi, miru, mita, miû, *&c.*
Ni, niru, nita, niû, *&c.*
Sughi, sughuru, sughita, sughiû, *&c.*

### Formation of the Verbs of the Second Conjugation

*All the roots of second conjugation verbs end in* I. *There are eight final syllables for these verbs; i.e.,* Bi, Chi, Ghi, Ki, Mi, Ni, Ri, Xi. *It is by these syllables that the verbs of the second conjugation (except for those mentioned above as being in the first conjugation) are recognized, and from which the tenses are formed.*

*The roots ending in the syllables* Bi, Ghi, Ki, Mi, *and* Ri *change the* I *to* V *for the present tense; e.g.,* Tobi, tobu; Coghi, coghu; Caki, caku; Yomi, yomu; Kiri, kiru.

*Those ending in* Chi *change to* Tçu *for the present; e.g.,* Mochi, motçu; Cachi, catçu; Tachi, tatçu.

*Those ending in* Ni *change to* Nuru *for the present; e.g.,* Xini, xinuru; Yni, ynuru.[28]

*Those ending in* Xi *change to* Su *for the present; e.g.,* Fanaxi, fanasu*;* Cudaxi, cudasu*;* Taraxi, tarasu.

*For the preterit those ending* Obi *and* Omi *change to* ôda*; e.g.,* Yomi, yôda*;* Tobi, tôda*;* Yobi, yôda*;* Yorocobi, yorocôda. Tomi *becomes* tonda.

*Those ending in* Abi *and* Ami *change to* ŏda*; e.g.,* Yerabi, yerŏda*;* Vogami, vogŏda*;* Yami, yŏda.

*Those ending in* Imi *change to* ûda*; e.g.,* Najimi, najŭda*;* Nijimi, nijŭda*;* Ximi, xûda.[29]

*Those ending in* Umi *and* Ubi *change their endings to* Vnda *or in some instances* ûda. *While some have two forms others have only one form which is seen in use, the more general is* Vnda*; e.g.,* Musubi, musunda*;* Susumi, susunda *or* susûda*;* Nusumi, nusunda *or* nusûda*;* Sumi, sunda *or* sûda*;* Cumi, cunda *only.*

*Those ending in* Ebi *and* Emi *change to* Eôda*; e.g.,* Sakebi, sakeôda*;* Sonemi, soneôda.

*Those ending in* Ghi *change to* Ida*; e.g.,* Auoghi, auoida*;* Voyoghi, voyoida*;* Coghi, coida.

*Those ending in* Ni *change to* Inda*; e.g.,* Xini, xinda*;* Yni, ynda.

*Those ending in* Chi *and* Ri *change to* Tta*; e.g.,* Machi, matta*;* Cachi, catta*;* Tachi, tatta*;* Kiri, kitta*;* Chiri, chitta*;* Cari, catta.

*Those ending in* Ki *and* Xi *change to* Ita*; e.g.,* Caki, caita*;* Faki, faita*;* Nuki, nuita*;* Todoki, todoita*;* Sosoki, sosoita*;* Saxi, saita*;* Fataxi, fataita*;* Maxi, maita *or* maxita*;* Coxi, coita *or* oxita. *The following add* Ta *to the root; e.g.,* Moxi, moxita*;* Muxi, muxita*;* Fuxi, fuxita*;* Mexi, mexita.

*The future can be formed in two ways. The first and more common way is to change* I *to* ŏ, ŏzu, *or* ŏzuru*; e.g.,* Yomi, yomŏ, yomŏzu, yomŏzuru*;* Yerabi, yerabŏ, *etc.;* Kiri, kirŏ*;* Xini, xinŏ*;* Auoghi, auogŏ.[30] *Those ending in* Chi *change to* Tŏ*; e.g.,* Cachi, catŏ, *etc.;* machi, matŏ. *Those ending in* Xi *change to* Sŏ*; e.g.,* Mŏxi, mŏsŏ*;* Nagaxi, nagasŏ*;* Mexi, mesŏ*;* Coxi, cosŏ, *etc. The other way, which is easy too, is to change the final* V *of the present indicative to* ŏ*; e.g.,* Yomu, yomŏ*;* Kiku, kikŏ*;* Mŏsu, mŏsŏ*;* Mesu, mesŏ. *Those ending in* çu *change to* Tŏ*; e.g.,* Tatçu, tatŏ*;* Catçu, catŏ. *Those ending in* Nuru *change to* Nŏ*; e.g.,* Xinuru, xinŏ*;* Ynuru, ynŏ. *This second rule seems to be more naturally in accord with the rules for the Japanese language.*

*The imperative changes the final* I *of the root to* E. *Those ending in* Chi *change to* Te*; e.g.,* Yome*;* Kike*;* Tamochi, tamote*;* Vchi, ute*;* Machi, mate.

*The present conjunctive is formed by adding* Ba *to the imperative; e.g.,* Yomeba*;* Tateba.[31] *For the preterit,* Reba *is added to the preterit indicative; e.g.,* Yôdarebe.[32] *For the future the final* Ru *of the future indicative is changed to* Reba*; e.g.,* Yomŏzureba. *The conjunctive in* Domo *is formed in the same manner; e.g.,* Yomedomo, yôdaredomo, yomŏzuredomo.

*The conditional is formed from the future indicative by changing the* ŏ *to* Aba*; e.g.,* Yomaba*;* Tataba.[33] *The preterit is formed by adding* Raba *to the indicative preterit; e.g.,* Yôdaraba*;* Tattaraba.[34]

*The preterit participle is formed from the preterit by changing the* A *to* E*; e.g.,* Yôde*;* Kite*;* Tatte. *The present participle, in* Te, *is formed by adding* Te *['hand'] to the root of any verb. This is properly a substantive and thus governs the genitive as do the other substantives. It does not indicate tense; e.g.,* Yomite*;* Cakite*;* Machite, *etc.*

*The negative present can be formed in two ways. The first, and that which accords with the rules for* Canadzucai, *is formed by changing* I *of the root to* Anu *or* Azu*; e.g.,* Corobi, corobanu, corobazu*;* Yomi, yomanu, *etc.;* Coghi, coghanu*;* Caki, cacanu*;*[35] Kiri, kiranu*;* ini, inanu. *Those ending in* Chi *change to* Tanu*; e.g.,* Tachi, tatanu. *Those ending in* Xi *change to* Sanu*; e.g.,* Fanasanu. *Another formation common to all is made with the future indicative by changing* ŏ *to* Anu *or* Azu*; e.g.,* Corobŏ, corobanu, corobazu*;* Yomŏ, yomanu, *etc.;* Coghŏ, coghanu*;* Cakŏ, cakanu*;* Kirŏ, kiranu*;* Inŏ, inanu*;* Tatŏ, tatanu*;* Matŏ, matanu*;* Fanasŏ, fanasanu. *This rule is common to all three conjugations by changing the affirmative future indicative* ŏ *to* Anu *and the* ô *and* û *to* Nu *or* Zu*;*[36] *e.g.,* Todomeô, todomenu, todomezu*;* Saxeô, saxenu, *etc.;* Tateô, tatenu*;* Miû, minu*;* Yomŏ, yomanu*;* Tatŏ, tatanu*;* Fanasŏ, fanasanu*;* Narauŏ, narananu*;* Vomouŏ, vomouanu*;* Furuuo, furuuanu. *For the second conjugation preterit, those in* Nu *are changed to* Nanda*: e.g.,* Yomananda. *For the preterit participle* Da *is changed to* De*; e.g.,* Yomanande. *For the second form of the negative participle, the* Nu *is changed to* Ide*; e.g.,* Yomaide, Corobaide, Tataide, Totonouaide. *For the future the particle* majij[37] *or* mai *is added to the affirmative present indicative; e.g.,* Yomumajij, yomumai*;* Matçumajij, matçumai.

### Formation of the Third Conjugation and the Roots from Which the Tenses Are Formed

*The final syllables of the third conjugation are the diphthongs* Ai, Oi, Vi. *By these syllables the verbs are known to belong to this conjugation, and from them the tenses are formed. The present indicative is formed by changing* Ai *to* ŏ, Oi *to* ô, *and* Vi *to* û*; e.g.,* Narai, narŏ*;* Vomoi, vomô*;* furui, furû. *The preterit is formed by adding the syllable*

Ta *to the present; e.g.,* Narŏta, Vomôta, Furûta. *The future is formed by changing the final* I *of the root to* Vŏ, vŏzu, vŏzuru*; e.g.,* Narauŏ, narauŏzu, *etc.;* Vomouŏ, vomouŏzu, *etc.;* Furuuŏ, furuuŏzu, *etc. The present imperative is formed by changing the final* I *to* Ye*; e.g.,* Naraye, Vomoye, Furuye.

*For the present conjunctive* Ba *or* Domo *is added to the imperative; e.g.,* Narayeba, narayedomo*;* Vomoyeba, vomoyedomo*;* Furuyeba, furuyedomo. *For the preterit* Reba *or* Redamo[38] *is added to the indicative preterit; e.g.,* Narŏtareba, narŏtaredomo*;* Vomôtareba, vomôtaredomo*;* Furûtareba, furûtaredomo.

*The present conditional is formed by changing* ŏ *of the future to* Aba*; e.g.,* Narauaba, Vomouaba, Furuuaba. *The preterit is formed by adding* Raba *to the indicative preterit; e.g.,* Narŏtaraba, Vomôtaraba, Furûtaraba.

*The negative present is formed by changing the* I *of the root to* Vanu *or* vazu*; e.g.,* Narai, narauanu, narauazu*;* Vomoi, vomouanu, *etc.;* Furui, Furuuana, *etc. This form can also be formed from the future by changing the* ŏ *to* Anu *or* azu*; e.g.,* Narauŏ, narananu, *etc. For the preterit the* Nu *is changed to* Nanda*; e.g.,* Narauananda. *For the preterit participle the* Da *is changed to* De*; e.g.,* Narauanande. *For the second form the* Nu *of the present is changed to* Ide*; e.g.,* Narauaide, Vomouaide, Furuuaide. *For the future the particle* Majii,[39] maji, *or* mai *is added to the affirmative present indicative;* e.g., Narŏmajii, narŏmaji, narŏmai*;* Vomômajii, ji, *or* mai*;* Furûmajii, ji, *or* mai.

*The verb* Yy *'to speak' becomes* Yû, yûta, yuŏ, yye, yuanu. Yei *or* yoi *'to become sick' becomes* Yô, yôta, youŏ, yoye, yonanu. *The substantive verb* Saburai, *which also belongs to this conjugation, becomes* Saburŏ, saburauanu*; and* Sŏrai *becomes* Sŏrŏ, soro, sŏraite, sŏraye, sorouanu.

Rodriguez follows these formational rules with a full display of all the forms of the three conjugations. In his display he, like Alvarez before him, recapitulates the appropriate rules for each form. Collado nowhere presents his conjugational system as a paradigm but does, as we shall see, include a full complement of example sentences in his description, something which Rodriguez does not do in the *Arte Breve*.

*Bibliography*

In the examination of any portion of the Christian materials certain works are indispensable. Father Johannes Laures, S.J., *Kirishitan Bunko* (Tokyo, 1957) remains the basic bibliographic source for the study of all sources of the Christian Century, while Hashimoto Shinkichi, *Kirishitan kyōgi no kenkyū* (Tokyo, 1929) and Doi Tadao, *Kirishitan gogaku no kenkyū* (Tokyo, 1942) serve as indespensible guides to our understanding of the linguistic aspects of the field. A later contribution to the general bibliography has been made by Fukushima Kunimichi, *Kirishitan shiryō to kokugo kenkyū* (Tokyo, 1973).

The basic grammatical study of the period, based upon the *shōmono* materials, is Yuzawa Kōkichirō, *Muromachi jidai gengo no kenkyū* (Tokyo, 1958). More closely related to the language reflected in the text is his "Amakusabon Heike monogatari no gohō," in *Kyōiku ronbunshū* (no. 539, Jan. 1929). An English treatment of the grammatical system of the period is to be found in R. L. Spear, "A Grammatical Study of *Esopo no Fabulas*," an unpublished doctoral thesis (Michigan, 1966). The phonology has been carefully analyzed by Ōtomo Shin'ichi, *Muromachi jidai no kokugo onsei no kenkyū* (Tokyo, 1963), with a valuable contribution made in English by J. F. Moran, "A Commentary on the *Arte Breve da Lingoa Iapao* of João Rodriguez, S.J., with Particular Reference to Pronunciation," an unpublished doctoral thesis (Oxford, 1971). This latter work presents an exhaustive examination of the phonological system reflected in the *Arte Breve* of 1620 within the framework of Berhard Bloch's phonemic theory.

Two lexical works have been used as basic references in this translation. The *Vocabulario de Lingoa de Iapam* (hereafter the *Vocabulario*) produced by the Jesuit Mission Press at Nagasaki in the years 1603 and 04. In a carefully annotated version by Professor Doi, under the title *Nippo jisho* (Tokyo, 1960), this work is the most important single source for the vocabulary of the period. The second work is the *Dictionarium sive Thesauri Linguae Iaponicae Compendium* (hereafter the *Dictionarium*) which is the companion piece to the present text. This dictionary has been carefully edited and cross-referenced by Ōtsuka Mitsunobu, under the title *Koriyaado Ra Su Nichi jiten* (Tokyo, 1966). In this form it has served as a constant aid to the translator in the determination of the proper glosses for the lexical items in the text.

The aforementioned *Arte* of 1604-08 by Rodriguez, has been the single most frequently used tool in the preparation of this translation.[40] As the most significant influence upon Collado's work and the source for most of his material, both theoretical and practical, I have related the two works at every point in the translation. In its Japanese version by Professor Doi, *Rodorigesu Nihon daibunten* (Tokyo, 1950), this work has been invaluable in gaining a clearer understanding of many of the passages which might have otherwise been obscure.

Rodriguez' *Arte Breve* of 1620, while having no influence upon the preparation of the *Ars Grammaticae*, is nevertheless of fundamental importance as a work against which Collado's treatment of Japanese grammar is to be judged. This shorter grammar is as yet to be fully translated into English—Moran having limited his study to the treatment of the phonology.

With respect to the text itself I have made this translation on the basis of the facsimile edition published by the Tenri Central Library in 1972 as part of its *Classica Japonica* series. Ōtsuka Takanobu, *Koiyaado-cho Nihongo bunten* (Tokyo, 1934) and its revised edition under the title of *Koriyaado Nihon bunten* (Tokyo, 1957) have served as invaluable aids at every step of the translation.

Ōtsuka's second edition is of invaluable scholarly importance because it contains a cross-reference to the Spanish manuscript from which Collado prepared the printed Latin edition as well as a concordance to the Japanese vocabulary.[41] This translation attempts to supplement Ōtsuka's invaluable contribution by relating the Latin text of this grammar with Rodriguez' *Arte*.

*Editorial Conventions*

The Latin matrix of the text is printed in italic letters while the Japanese is in roman. For this translation I have reversed the convention. (In footnotes where the text is quoted the style of the original is followed.) In making editorial corrections in the Japanese material the corrected version is presented in brackets with periods to indicate the general location;

e.g., *mairu mai queredomo* [... qeredomo]

(The only exception to this rule is the correcting of a missing open *o*, q.v.) Sentences that have been taken from the *Arte* are indicated by the parenthetical recording of the leaf number of the citation immediately after the sentence;

e.g., *xô tame no chôqui gia* (22) 'it is....

Shorter sentences and specific words that in all likelihood have been taken from the *Arte* are not listed if they are to be found in the section elsewhere noted as being the source of the material covered. Any significant alteration in the form of the source is noted. Since the *Arte* is numbered by the leaf, *v* is added to the number to indicate the *verso*.

All the corrections made by the *errata* (on page 75 of the text) have been applied to the text without notation unless the correction is itself in error.

The punctuation follows the text with the following exceptions;

1. In translating from Latin the English follows modern rules of punctuation.

2. Single quotes have been introduced into the text to mark glosses and translations.

3. In transcribing the Japanese citations any alteration of the original punctuation is noted.

4. The spacing of words in Japanese—a relatively casual matter in the text—has been regularized on the basis of the predominant pattern.

5. Two specific rules, based upon Collado's more or less consistent usage, are followed in the citing of verb forms:

a. In the most frequent citation of verbs, where the root form is followed by the present indicative ending, a comma is used;

e.g., *ari,u; ague,uru; mochi,tçu*

b. In an alternate form of citation, where the two forms are given in their entirety, a colon is used;

e.g., *ari:aru; ague:aguru; mochi:motçu*

Spelling and accentuation are treated in the following manner:

1. The *ſ* in all instances is represented by *s*.

2. The usage of *v* and *u* has been regularized: the *v* serves as the consonant; and *u* as the vowel, semi-vowel, and orthographic symbol; e.g., *vaga, uie, quan*, and *agueta*.

3. The predictable nasalization—marked by a tilde in the text—has not been included in the translation unless the presence of nasalization is morphologically significant; e.g., *tobu:tõda*.

4. The accent grave—which appears in no discernible pattern—is not transcribed in the translation.

5. The accent acute is used in the translation to mark the long *ú* [u:] and the long, open *ó* [ɔ:], in those places where the length is marked by Collado. Since the most frequent typographical error in the text is the failure to mark the presence of these long syllables, I follow the convention of correcting the absence of this feature in the Latin text by using the inverted caret in the translation. Thus, the appearance in the translation of *mósu* indicates that Collado recorded the length of this word, either by an accent acute (e.g., *mósu*), or an inverted caret (e.g., *mǒsu*). The appearance of *mǒsu* indicates that he did not, and that its absence is being corrected. The form *mǒsu* in the translation is therefore the shorthand equivalent for what would more regularly be *mosu* [*mósu*].

6. The circumflex, which indicates the long, closed *ô* [o:], is corrected as other errors by placing the corrected version of the item in brackets; e.g., *roppio* [*roppiô*].

---

## Prologue to the Reader

*With Some Advice on the Correct Pronunciation of the Japanese Language*

Long ago, at the beginning of the establishment of our orthodox faith in the Japanese kingdom, a grammar of this language was made by Father Ioannus Rodriguez of the Society of Jesus.[42] However, since things rarely turn out perfect at first attempt, and, because of the passing years that have made it difficult to find a copy of this grammar; I thought that it would honor God and the ministers who preach the faith (which cannot be taught without the use of language) if I were to select examples (and there are many) that are useful to this language, neglect those not accepted by the experts of the language, add, with the help of God (who gives words to the evangelists), the words that I have learned from experience, practice, and continuous reading, and by such means offer up a handbook of the Japanese language in which I would bring together in a brief span these examples with those precepts which the preachers (for whom I began this work) need to learn of the Japanese language. This is done because examples are necessary with the rules and precepts so that it is possible to demonstrate the rule which has just been explained. Not only have these examples been selected for the greater help and enjoyment of the students, but also their explanation has been added in Latin (which is the language most common to theologians); thus the teacher will have very little left to be desired. Even if all the elements included in this grammar, as in the dictionary (which with the help of God I plan to publish shortly),[43] are polished enough and sure enough to be used with trust; I would still want them to be submitted to the judgement of the reader so that the preaching of the faith, carried on with a more correct language, may become more fruitful.

When two vowels follow each other in any Japanese word, they are not pronounced as in the Latin word *valeo* or in the Spanish, *vaca*, but each is pronounced independently; *v*, *a*; *v*, *o*; *v*, *i*.

The letter *s* is pronounced as *sç*; e.g., *susumuru*, *sçusçumuru*.

The letter *j* is pronounced smoothly (*blande*), as in the Portuguese *joaõ* and *judeo*.

The letter *x* is also pronounced smoothly, as in the Portuguese (4 *queixumes*.

When there is the sign ˆ over the letter *o* it is pronounced *ou* with the lips almost closed and the mouth partly closed; e.g., *buppô*.

When there is the sign ˇ or ´ over the letter *o* it is pronounced with the mouth open as if there were two letters, *oo*; e.g., *tenxó* or *gacuxŏ*.[44]

If the signs we have just shown are over the letter *u*, it is pronounced long as if there were two letters, *uu*; e.g., *taifú* or *aiaŭ*.

When the sign ˜ is over the vowel, the sign should be pronounced like an *n*, not strongly but swiftly (*cursim*) and softly (*leniter*); e.g., *vãga*.[45]

*Qe* and *Qi* are written without *u*, because when *u* follows *q* or *c* both letters are pronounced as a *sinalepha*;[46] e.g., *quódai* or *quainin*.

When *u* follows *g* and immediately after the *u* is the letter *e* or *i*, it should be pronounced as in the Spanish word *guenin*; but if the letter *e* or *i* follows *g* immediately without the *u*, it should be pronounced as in the Italian word *giorno*; e.g., *xitãgi*.

The letter *z* is pronounced with the same strength as in the Spanish word *zumbar*; e.g., *mizu*.

But if there are two *zz* then they are pronounced more strongly; *e.g., mizzu*.

When there are two *tt*, *xx*, *zz*, *qq*, *cq*, *ij*, or *pp*[47] it is important to persist in order to obtain perfect pronunciation and the exact value of the word; for *mizu* means 'honey' and *mizzu* means 'water.' Therefore, if the words are said with the same strength or the same gentleness they can mean either 'water' or 'honey.'

When *ch* comes before a vowel it is pronounced as in the Spanish *chimera*; e.g., *fochó*.

But if *nh* comes before a vowel it is pronounced as in the Spanish *maña*; e.g., *nhuva*.

The letter *f* is pronounced in various regions of Japan as it is in Latin. In others it is pronounced as if it were an imperfect *h*. For both pronunciations the lips and the mouth should be nearly, but not completely, closed.

When *tç* is in a word (and it appears quite frequently) the student should pray that God have mercy on his pronunciation because the word is very difficult, and its pronunciation is not to be found (5 in any other language. It is not truly pronounced *tç*, nor as *s*, nor as *c* alone, but rather by striking the tongue violently against the teeth in order to pronounce both *t* and *ç*, but with more *ç* than *t* seeming to be sounded; e.g., *tçutçumu*.

The letter *r* is said smoothly and softly everywhere it is found, either at the beginning or in the middle of a word; e.g., *ranguió*, or *cutabiruru*.

*Ya*, *ye*, *yo*, and *yu* are pronounced as in Spanish.[48]

When words ending in *i* or *u* are pronounced by the Japanese, the last letter is almost not heard by the student. For instance, if he hears *gozaru* he will think he hears *gozar*, if he hears *fitotçu* he will believe he hears only *fitotç*, and when he hears *axi no fara* he will perceive only *ax no fara*.

When a word ending in a vowel is followed immediately by a consonant, particularly *b* or *s*,[49] between that vowel and consonant is pronounced the letter *n*, not perfectly, but softly; e.g., *sonõ gotoqu*.

I have given special care to the accenting of words.[50] This has been done so that the signs that have been placed correctly over the accented letter will allow the listener to understand the meaning of the words and the sentences of the speaker. For instance, *qèixèi* has the accent on both *èè*; *fibicàxi* has it on the first *i* and on the *a*.[51] This same arrangement will be respected in the dictionary, with the accent being written with the same degree of correctness as is able to be achieved with great attention. If at times I have made mistakes, I am prepared to correct them immediately. Concerning what has been explained too briefly or left out of this grammar and the dictionary, learned people will be able to do that when they add a third dictionary and a third grammar, since it is easy to supply this material. Because I wish neither to be criticized by the Head of our Order (*pater familias*) and the Lord our God, nor do I wish this knowledge to be wrapped up in a handkerchief;[52] I want by these two works to help and to cooperate in the salvation of the Japanese not only by preaching but also by offering to the preachers, if I can, the tools of the language and chiefly the method by which they might better learn the Japanese language, a task made very difficult by the persecutions in Japan. Farewell, Reader, and be of good cheer. Madrid, 30 August 1631.

---

(6

## In This Grammar We Have for the Most Part Observed the Arrangement Which Antonius Nebrissensis and Others Have Followed in Latin for the Treatment of Sentences, Namely Nouns, Pronouns, Etc.

### *The Noun—Its Declension and Its Gender*

In the Japanese language there are no case declensions as there are in Latin; but there are certain particles, which when suffixed to nouns, determine the differences between the cases for both common and proper nouns. The particles which form the nominative are five; *va*, *ga*, *cara*, *no*, and *iori*. The particle *va* is used when we want to give a sort of reduplicative[53] and specific turn to the person or thing that is signified by such a noun. It indicates either the first, second, or third person; e.g., *Vatacuxi va mairanu* 'I, or those related to me, will not come.' The particle *no* is suffixed to the second and third person, especially if they are inferior in rank or in a sentence where there is a relative construction which does not indicate a transitive action; e.g., *sonata no móxita coto* 'that which you said.' The particle *no* is also used when some indefinite form is used; e.g., *iie no aru ca miió* [... *miio*] 'see if there are houses.' The particle *ga* is used usually for the first and third persons of inferior status as well as for the second person when he is the most lowly or is to be humiliated; e.g., *Pedro ga qita* 'Peter came.' This particle is also used to indicate something indefinite, as has been said of the particle *no*; e.g., *coco ni va iie ga nai ca?* 'aren't the houses here?' It is also used in sentences that have a relative construction which does not indicate a transitive action. If the reference is to something of inferior or humble status the particle *ga* is also used; e.g., *soregaxi ga caita fumi* 'the letter which I wrote,' *sochi ga iúta coto* 'what you said.' The particles *cara* and *iori* are used to form the nominative case when the sentence shows a transitive action, especially if the sentence contains a relative construction; e.g., *Deus iori cudasareta gracia* 'the mercy which God gave,' *tono cara core vo vôxe tçuqerareta* 'the Lord taught this.' Sometimes the words are in the nominative case without any particle; e.g., *Pedro Ioaõ vo iobareta* 'Peter called (7 John.' There are two particles for the genitive; i.e., *no* and *ga*. The particle *no* is used for all persons of superior rank; e.g., *Padre no võ qiru mono* 'the priest's clothes, or habit.' The particle *ga* is used for people of inferior rank; e.g., *Pedro ga fumi* 'Peter's letter,' *sochi ga mono* 'your thing,' *are ga cane* 'your money,' *tono va iocu ga fucai fito gia* 'the Lord is of great cupidity, that is to say he is very eager.' Sometimes the particle *to* is suffixed to the genitive; e.g., *Pedro no to degozaru* 'it belongs to Peter.' But since this is not a perfect way of speaking, it is better not to use it. I have cited it so that if you hear it you will understand. When two nouns are joined to form a single word, the one which is like an adjective does not require the genitive particle; e.g., *cocuxu* 'the Lord of the kingdom.' According to the ordinary rule we should say *cocu no xu*. This way of forming the genitive is very common in Japanese; e.g., *Maria coto* 'Mary's thing.'

Two particles form the dative; i.e., *ni* and *ie*. For example, *Pedro ni móxita* 'I told Peter,' *Padre ie ague maraxita* 'I gave, or offered, it to the priest.'

There are five particles which form the accusative case; i.e., *vo, voba, va, ie,* and *ga*. The first, *vo,* is the most used; e.g., *Pedro vo iobe* 'call Peter.' *Va* is used when one wishes to express in particular a noun in the accusative; e.g., *niffon guchi va xiranu*[54] 'I don't know Japanese.' The ending *voba* is the same as *vo va,* changing the second *v* to *b* they use it as *va*; e.g., *fune voba nori sutete; cane bacari tori maraxita* 'abandoning ship, I took only money, or gold, with me.' *Ie* is used to indicate the place to which one goes; e.g., *Roma ie mairó* 'I go to Rome.' *Ga* is used for nouns which indicate non-living or humble things; e.g., *are ie gozare, mono ga móxitai* 'go there! I have something to tell you.' The accusative is also formed without any particle, as has been shown in the example second before last, where the second accusative is without a particle.

The vocative is formed with the particle *icani*. It is not suffixed to words as are the other particles but it is prefixed instead; e.g., *icani qimi core vo goronjerarei* 'look at this, My Lord.'[55] Usually, however, the vocative is formed without any particle; e.g., *Padre sama* (8 *qicaxerareio* 'listen, Reverend Father.'

There are three particles for the ablative; i.e., *iori*, *cara*, and *ni*. The third indicates the place in which; e.g., *iglesia ni gozaru* 'he is in church.' Sometimes *ni* is used after *no*; e.g., *sonata no ni xi aru ca?* 'are you going to make it yours, or take it for yours?' But this seems much more a dative than an ablative. The particles *cara* and *iori* are more common in the formation of the ablative; e.g., *Madrid cara maitta* 'I came from Madrid,' *Pedro iori corosareta* 'he was killed by Peter.'

There are four particles used to form the plural. They are placed immediately after the noun they pluralize and before the particles which indicate case. These four particles are *tachi*, *xu*, *domo*, and *ra*. The first, *tachi*, forms the plural of those noble things which one wishes to honor; e.g., *tono tachi* 'lords.' The particle *xu* forms the plural for noble things but not those of the highest rank; e.g., *samurai xu* 'nobles (*nobiles*), but not lords (*domini*).' The particle *domo* is suffixed to words which indicate humble things, either abstract, animate, or inanimate; e.g., *fiacuxó domo* 'farmer,' *ixi domo* 'stones,' *mma domo* 'horses.' The particle *ra* forms the plural of nouns which indicate very low things which are to be despised; e.g., *Iudeo ra* 'Jews.'[56] The case particles which are required by the sentence are placed after the pluralizing particles; e.g., *tono tachi no coto domo vo varú iú na* 'don't speak badly about the Lords' affairs.'

There are some words that are plural in themselves; e.g., *tomo gara* means 'men,' *Nan ban mono* 'European things,' *Nan ban mono vo fomuru na* 'don't praise European things.'

The particle *icani*, which as has been indicated above forms the vocative, is not placed after but always before the pronouns which are made plural, while the particles which form the plural are placed after; e.g., *icani Padre tachi vo qiqi nasare io* 'listen to the priests.'

But two of the four particles which form the plural, *domo* and *ra*, are with certain words singular. *Varera* and *midomo* mean 'I.' Sometimes both are found together in the singular; e.g., *midomora* 'I,' *midomora ga* 'my, or mine.' The particles *domo* and *ra* are also (9 suffixed to the singular when one wishes to humiliate the thing mentioned; e.g., *hara domo ga itai* 'I have a stomach ache,' *asu domo va aru mai* 'tomorrow will not come,' *asu ra va naró mode* 'tomorrow will perhaps not come.'

The particle *va* is suffixed to singular and plural nouns which already have a particle; e.g., *coco ie va mairanu* 'he will not come here,' *coco cara va denu* 'he did not go out from here,' *coco ni va aru mai* 'he will not enter here.' Sometimes *va* replaces the particles of the declension; e.g., *fune de saie ióió tçuita ni, cachi va nacanaca naru mai* (119v) 'I arrived with such difficulty by ship: I would undoubtedly never have arrived had I come by foot, or on foot.'[57] The particle *va* here replaces *cara*.

Japanese does not have the genders feminine, masculine, and neuter as Latin does. There are, however, certain nouns which are feminine or masculine because of their meaning. Other nouns are common to both these genders. For things which do not have a proper gender *vo* is placed before masculine nouns and *me* before feminine; e.g., *voivo* means 'male fish' and *meivo* 'female fish,' *vojica* means 'roe-buck,' *melica* [*mejica*] 'roe-doe,'[58] *coma* means 'horse,' *zoiacu* 'mare,' *xô* means 'male hawk,' *dai* 'female hawk,' *cotoi* means 'bull,' *meuxi* 'cow,' *votoco* means 'man,' *vonago*, *nhóbó*, or *vonna* 'woman.' All these words are placed in the dictionary as they come to mind.

The nominal adjectives have no gender or declension but make use of the same particles as the nouns. There are however many and diverse adjectives. Certain ones end in *ai* others in *oi*, *ei*, *ui* and *ij*. There are other, more proper adjectives, which are formed by adding *no* to nouns. When the first five types of adjectives are placed before nouns they are then properly adjectives and do not in any way alter the composition of the sentence. But when they are placed after nouns they become more like verbs and are in fact conjugated like them; e.g., *tacai iama* 'a high mountain,' *xiguei ideiri* 'frequent comings and goings,' *caxicoi* (10 *fito* 'a wise man,' *cavaij mono* 'a wretched thing,' *aiaui coto* 'a dangerous thing,' *umare tçuqi no cuchi* 'one's natural, or mother tongue.' There are also adjectives ending in *na* which, when they are placed before nouns, do not alter the construction; e.g., *qirei na coto* 'a clean thing.' All the adjectives, except those ending in *no*, change their form in some way when they occur before verbs. Those that end in *ai* change to *ó*; e.g., *cono iama va tacó gozaru* 'this mountain is lofty.' Those ending in *ei* change to *eô*; e.g., *cono iama va xigueô gozaru* 'these mountains are dense.' Those ending in *oi* change to *ô*; e.g., *caxicô gozaru* 'he is wise.' Those ending in *ui* change to *ú*; e.g., *xei no ficú gozaru* 'he is small in stature.' Those ending in *ii* [*ij*] change to *iú*; e.g., *caiú gozaru* 'it itches.'[59] Among those adjectives ending in *ij* there are many which come from verbs; e.g., *nozomi,u* means 'to wish,' and from it comes *nozomaxij* 'which is to be wished for.' Other adjectives come from nouns; e.g., *varambe* means 'a child, or infant,' and from this comes *varamberaxij* which means 'childish.' Other examples may be found in the dictionary.

Adjectives which end in *na* change the *na* to *ni* when they are placed before verbs; e.g., *fuxin ni zonzuru* 'I think it doubtful.' The adjectives that end in *no* sometimes change the *no* to *na*; e.g., *bechi no fito* changes to *bechi na fito* 'a different man.' Sometimes when it is followed by a verb the *na* changes to a *ni*; e.g., *bechi ni gozaru* 'it is different.' However, the meaning remains the same whether the word ends in *na* or *no*; e.g., *bechi no fito no cuhi cara qiita* [... *cuchi* ...] is the same as *bechi na fito no cuchi cara qiita* 'I heard it from the mouth of a different person.'[60] The only difference in these forms is that when the word ends in *no* no change occurs as a consequence of what follows. But, as has been said, those adjectives that end in *na* change to *ni* when they come before a verb. If a substantive verb follows an adjective, it is an elegant statement; e.g., *cono iami va tacó gozaru* 'this mountain is high.' But if this kind of verb does not follow, the sense is not altered since the adjective is used as a substantive verb. But this is not used before superiors. To them we will not say *cono iama va tacai* but rather *cono iama va tacó gozaru*. The same is true for the other adjectives.

Adjectives usually end in *i* but infrequently these adjectives change to *xi* or to *qu*. *Ioi*, which means 'good,' changes to *ioqu*, or *ioxi*; e.g., *ioqu dancó xite*, which has the meaning of 'offering good (11 council.'[61] There are innumerable nouns which become adjectives if *na* is suffixed to them; e.g., *afo* means 'ignorance' and from it comes the word *afo na* which means 'ignorant,' *jiiu* means 'liberty' and *jiiu na* means 'which is free.' Other examples are offered by the dictionary.

There are certain abstract nouns which become adjectives when they precede a vocable (*vocabulis*) with the meaning of 'man'; e.g., *jifi* means 'pity,' but when the word *jin* is placed after it, it becomes *jifijin* 'a pitiable person.' *Fin* means 'poverty,' but when the word *nin* is suffixed to it, it becomes *finnin* 'a poor person.' In the same way, when one suffixes *ja* to *fin*, it makes *finja*, which also means 'a poor person.' The word *ban* means 'watch,' but if the word *ja* is added to it, it becomes *banja* 'a careful person.' Many other examples can be found in the dictionary.

There are in Japanese certain words which are borrowed from Chinese, called *cobita*[62] or *coie*, and are written together to form by their union a noun and an adjective. Thus, *ten* mean 'heaven,' *xu* means 'lord,' and *tenxu* means 'lord of heaven.'

The preterit of verbs (which will be taken up in their place) seem to have the same strength and meaning as adjectives when they are used before nouns; e.g., *iogoreta te* 'dirty hands,' where *iogoreta* is the preterit of the verb *iogore,uru* 'I became dirty.' *Caita qió* means 'a written book' and *caita* is the preterit of the verb *caqi,u* I write.' The abstract (*abstracta*), or root from which the verb is formed, is itself a noun which signifies the action of the verb in the abstract; e.g., *facari* means 'measure,' and it comes from the verb *facari,u* 'I measure' while *fajime* means 'beginning,' and comes from the verb *fajime,uru* 'I begin.' Others will be found in the dictionary. The prepositional particle *mono*, when placed before an abstract or verbal noun, forms a noun which indicates the subject who does the action; e.g., *mono* before *caqi* makes *monocaqi* 'one who writes.' This same particle when placed after a root forms a noun which indicates the effect of an action; e.g., *caqimono* 'a writing.'

The particle *goto* placed after these same roots forms a noun (12 which means a thing which is worthy of the action indicated by the verb; e.g., *mi* is the root of the verb *mi,uru* 'I see,' and *migoto* is 'a visible thing, or a thing worthy of being seen'; while *qiqi* is the root of the verb *qiqi,u* 'I hear,' and *qiqigoto* means 'a thing which can be heard, or is worthy of being heard.'

If we place certain substantive nouns after certain of the verbal nouns about which we have been speaking, there is formed a noun which has the meaning of the action; e.g., *foxi* is the root of the verb *foxi,u* 'to dry under the sun'; but, if *ivo* 'fish' is placed after it, the meaning of the expression *foxiivo* becomes 'fish dried in the sun.'

When the particle *dógu* 'instrument' is placed after the root of a verb it forms a noun meaning the cause or instrument of the action indicated by the verb; e.g., *varaidógu* 'the cause, or instrument of ridicule,' *caqidógu* 'a writing instrument, or an instrument for writing.'

The particle *me* when suffixed to a verb forms a noun which indicates the terminus of the action; e.g., *avaxe* is the root of the verb *avaxe,uru* 'to unite or join two things,' and *avaxeme* means 'junction.' The same is true of other forms.

An abstract noun can be formed from those adjectives ending in *i* if the *i* is changed to *sa*; e.g., *nagai* means 'is long,' and *nagasa* means 'length.' The adjectives ending in *na* change the *na* to *sa* in order to form abstract nouns; e.g., *aqiraca na* which means 'clear' will become *aqiracasa* 'clarity.'

Sometimes from two nouns taken together, often with a change in the first or last letter, there is formed a third noun, which is quasi-descriptive (*quasi connotativus*), almost like an adjective or noun with a genitive; e.g., from *qi* 'wood' and *fotoqe* 'idol' there results *qibotoqe* 'wooden idol,' with the *f* changed to *p* [*b*]. But if the prefixed noun ends in *e*, this *e* is changed to *a* in the attributive of the compound; e.g., *tçumasaqi* 'the tip of the nail,' *canacugui* 'iron nails.' A word which is placed second in these compounds may change its first letter; if it is *f* it becomes *b* or *p*, if it is *s* it becomes *z*, if it is *c* it becomes *g*, if it is *tç* it becomes *zz*, if it is *x* it becomes *j*; e.g., *caribune*, *buppô*, (13 *nigorizaqe*, *soragoto*, *qizzumari*, and *sorajeimon*. See the dictionary.

## *Pronouns*

In the Japanese language there are no derivative pronouns, such as *meus,a,um*, etc.; but the primitive pronouns, such as *mei*, *tui*, etc., are used. These primitive forms do not have declensions for case, but rather use the particles which are common to both nouns and pronouns.

Certain particles (about which we will speak later) when added to a word indicate honor and thereby form a pronoun or substitute for it in such circumstances as pronouns would normally be used. Thus, if I say *von fumi*, when speaking to someone else, it is immediately understood that I am speaking about his letter and not mine; for if I were speaking about mine I would not say *von fumi* but only *fumi*, since the particle *von*, which indicates honor, signifies 'your letter.' This is also true for such particles as *mi* which also attributes honor to the noun to which it is joined.

### *First Person Pronouns—Ego, etc.*[63]

There are eight particles which signify 'I, mine, to me, etc.' They are *vatacuxi, soregaxi, vare, mi, varera, midomo, midomora, vare.*[64] The first four indicate a degree of superiority on the part of those who use them. The others are more humble. Women use three other particles *mizzucara, varava*, and *vagami* which are not used by men. The people in the countryside use two others, *vara* [*vora*] and *vorara*, while priests when speaking of themselves use *gusô*, that is to say 'I, a worthless man of the cloth,' and old men when speaking of themselves use *guró*, 'I, a worthless and despicable old man.' The king (*rex*) says *chin* or *maru* which means 'I, the King.' (14

To form the plural of these pronouns the pluralizing particles *domo* or *ra* are added; e.g., *midomo ga maitta toqi* 'when we went.' To indicate the difference between the cases, the endings about which we have spoken are suffixed.

### *Second Person Pronouns—Tu, tui, tibi, etc.*[65]

There are many particles that form the second person pronoun. They are differentiated to indicate those persons deserving no honor and respect, those deserving some, moderate, great, or maximal honor and respect. In speaking to inferiors there are three particles used for 'you'; *vare, vonore*, and *sochi*. If *me* or *mega* is added as in *vareme* or *varemega* it means we very much despise the person being spoken to. If we speak to people who are on our own level, or just a little inferior, we use one of the three particles *sonata, sonofŏ*, or *varesama*. If we speak to a superior person, or someone on an equal level but with whom we must speak elegantly, we use one of the seven particles *conata, qixo, qifó, gofen, qiden, conatasama*, and *sonatasama*. When speaking to persons of high rank, if we place the name of their office before *sama*, it serves as a pronoun; e.g., *Padresama gozare* 'will the Father come.'

*Conata, cochi,* and *conofŏ* mean 'I, mine,' but in the distributive sense of 'from me, or what concerns me.' In the same way *sochi, sonofó,* and *sonata* mean 'you, from you, or what concerns you.'

The plurals are formed by adding the particles listed above to the pronouns according to the different degrees of honor. *Vonore domo, varera,* and *sochira* mean 'you' when speaking to inferiors. *Vare tachi* and *sonata domo* mean 'you' with persons of the same rank. *Qifó tachi, vocatagata,* and *vono vono* mean 'you' to persons requiring honor. The declension of these honorable expressions follows the declension (15 of common particles.

### *Third Person Pronouns—Ille, illa, illud*[66]

The two particles *care care* and *are are* mean 'this (*ille, illa, illud*)' when speaking of inferior things.[67] There are four particles; *aitçu, aitçume, areme,* and *caitçume* which mean 'this' when one wants to show disrespect for the things being spoken about. This idea is emphasized if one adds *ga* to those forms that end in *me*; e.g., *aitçuga* and *aitçumega* 'this humble man.' *Cono* means 'this (*hic, haec, hoc*),' *sono* means 'that (*iste, ista, istud*),' and *ano* means 'that (*ille, illa, illud*).' These words require a noun after them; e.g., *cono fito* 'this man' with *cono mono* having the same meaning but not being an honorific expression. *Sono coto* means 'that thing,' *ano fito* 'that person,' *conata* or *conofó* 'here,' *sonata* or *sonofó* 'there,' and *anofó* 'there, yonder.' *Core* means 'this (*hic*),' *sore* 'that (*istud*),' and *are* 'that (*illud*).' These forms are in the neuter gender and are not followed by nouns. Their plurals are *corera, sorera,* and *arera,* while the others follow the common rules. *Cano* means 'that which we have mentioned'; e.g., *cano fito* 'that person.' The pronoun 'a certain (*quidam*)' is made with the particle *aru*; e.g., *aru fito* 'a certain person,' *aru tocoro ni* 'in a certain place.'

The pronoun 'each (*unusquisque*)' is formed with the particles *men men* and *sore sore.*

The pronoun 'each and every (*universi & singuli*)' is formed with *tare mo mina.*

The pronoun 'anyone (*quicumque*)' is formed with *tare nite mo, tare nite mo are*, and *tare nari tomo*.

The particle *tare mo*, when placed before a negative, forms the pronoun 'no one, or nobody'; e.g., *tare mo mairananda* 'nobody went.' The particle *nani taru coto nari tomo* means 'whatever happens, or whichever thing happens.' The particle *mei mei* means 'to each, or everyone in particular.'

The particle *goto* makes the distributive pronoun meaning 'every.' This form is used after vocables which are proper to the Japanese language; i.e., *iomi*. The same results are achieved by placing the (16 particle *mai* before vocables which come from the Chinese language; i.e., *coie*. For example, *fi* means 'day,' and *figoto ni* means 'daily.' *Nen* is a Japanese borrowing from a Chinese word meaning 'year,' and *mainen* means 'every year, or all year.' The same result is obtained by the repetition of the noun; e.g., *fito* means 'person,' and *fitibito* means 'all the people, or many people,' *fi* means 'day,' and *fibi ni* means 'all of the days, or every day.'

The indefinite pronoun 'some (*aliqui*)' is formed with *niiotte*; e.g., *toqi niiotte* 'some times,' *fito niiotte* 'some men.'

The pronoun 'the same (*idem*)' is formed with *vonaji*; e.g., *vonaji tocoro cara* 'from the same place.' The particle *dôjen* means the same thing but in the neuter ; e.g., *dôjen degozaru* 'it is the same.' This word is used in reply to some one who has congratulated you, etc.

The pronoun 'himself (*ipse*)' is formed with the particles *nuxi, sono mi*, and *vaga*. The particle *vareto mi* forms the pronoun 'himself (*ipsemet*)'; e.g., *vareto mi ni ata vo nasu* (96) 'he brings harm to himself,' *mi vo vasurete; ta vo tasuquru* 'he forgets himself and saves others.' The particle *vatacuxi* means 'a thing which belongs to oneself (*re propria*)'; e.g., *vatacuxi no coto* 'ones own thing,' *vatacuxi ni ivareta* 'he spoke for himself.'

The pronoun 'somebody (*aliquis*)' is made with the particles *tare zo* and *taso*; e.g., *tare zo maittaraba* 'if somebody were to come,' *taso sacana ga aru ca tói ni iqe* [... *toi* ...] 'let someone go and ask if there is food.'

The neuter pronoun 'something (*aliquid*)' is formed with the particles *nan zo* and *nanica*; e.g., *nan zo ga araba cuvózu* 'I would eat if there were something,' *ima faia te ga jiiú ni gozaru fodo ni nanica caqi maraxô* 'I would write something if I were to have my hands free, or untied.'

The interrogative 'who (*quis*)' is translated with the three particles *tare, taga,* and *taso.* The particles *taga* or *tare no* form the genitive; e.g., *taga mono ca* 'whose thing is this.' When someone comes to the door and knocks, he says *mono mó.*[68] To this one responds *taso, taga,* or *tare* 'who is it?' *Nani* means 'what (*quid*)'; e.g., *nani vo suru* (17 *ca* or *nani goto vo suru ca?* 'what are you doing?' *nani ni sore vo totte iqu ca?* 'for what reason do you bring this to me?'

*Relative Pronouns*

The relative pronoun is formed by placing the noun, in connection with which there is a relative (*relativum*), after the verb; e.g., *ten ni maximasu varera ga von voia* 'Our Father who is in Heaven,' *deta tocoro va* 'the place from which he came out,' *te ni sumi no tçuita fito* (88) 'a man to whose hands ink is adhering.' If the sentence (*oratio*) requires a nominative before the verb it must be formed with one of the particles which indicate the nominative; *ga, no,* or *iori.* For example, *vatacuxi ga caita fumi* 'the letter which I wrote,' *conata no vôxerareta coto* 'the thing which Your Lordship says.' The third particle, *iori,* is used when there is movement in the sentence; e.g., *Deus iori ataie cudasareta gracia* 'the grace which God provided, or gave,' *ano tocoro ni amata no qió atta vo torareta* (87v.) 'he brought what many books there were in that place.' When two sentences containing a relation come together the first is placed second by general rule,[69] and the second uses either a past, present, or future particle according to what is required by the sense of the sentence; e.g., *qesa Oracio vo móxita qió ga tçucuie no uie ni aru vo motte coi* 'bring the book which is on the desk (*sedila*) at which I said my prayers this morning.' In this sentence *qió ga,* which is the first relative, comes after the verb *móxita*; and the *vo* which stands for the second relative comes after the verb *aru.* When we want to be more specific about that of which we are speaking we place the particle *tocoro no* between the thing itself and the verb; e.g., *vare to dôxin xita tocoro no mono domo va mina buguen ni natta* 'all those who agreed with me became rich.' Sometimes the relative, because of the difficulty in understanding it, is expressed by expositions (*per exponentes*). Thus, in place of *ima corosareta Pedro no co va sonata no chijn gia* which means 'the son of Peter who has just been killed was your friend,' we say *ima Pedro corosareta sono co va sonata no chijn de gozaru.*

Sometimes they join two particles, as determined by the case, and form a kind of relative pronoun which is placed before the relative; e.g., *sono tocoro de no dancó* 'the consultation at that place,' (18 *Marsella ie no fune* 'the ship to Marseille,' *maire to no móxi goto dearu* [ ... *gia*] 'it is said that I should go.'

*Mairu mai to no dancó ni qivamatta* 'it was resolved that he not go,' *maitte nochi no dancó* 'the consultation he arrived after,' *varambe cara no catagui* 'a custom from youth,' *xô tame no chôgui gia* (22) 'this is the plan (*ars*) according to which it will be done,' *anofito no vo toró* 'I shall take what belongs to that man.' This ends the note on relative pronouns.

### *The Formation of the Verb and Its Conjugation*[70]

The verbs in Japanese have no number or person. These distinctions are indicated instead by the particles used in the formation of the plurals and in the declensions. There are three affirmative conjugations and the same number of negative.

The root (*radix*) of the verb does not by itself indicate tense. For this reason it is necessary to conjugate the verb in order to show the tenses.

All the verbs of the first conjugation[71] end in *e*. Those ending in *gi* or *ji*, together with *xi* and *maraxi*, although they end in *i*, are also in the first conjugation. If the root ends in *de* or *gi*, the present form is made by changing them to *zzuru*; e.g., *fagi* forms its present in *fazzuru* and means 'to blush,' *de* becomes *zzuru* and means 'to leave.' If the root ends in *je* or *ji* it changes in the present to *zuru*; e.g., *maje:mazuru* 'to mix,' *anji:anzuru* 'to consider.' If they end in *xe* they change to *suru*; e.g., *avaxe:avasuru* 'to join.' *Xi* and *maraxi*, which (as we have said) are in the first conjugation,[72] change *xi* to *suru*; e.g., *xi:suru* 'to do,' *maraxi:marasuru* which also means 'to do.' If the root ends in *te* it changes to *tçuru*; e.g., *sodate:sodatçuru* 'to nourish, or support.' The remaining roots which end in *e* change, in their separate ways, the *e* to *uru*; e.g., *ague:aguru* 'to offer,' *nigue:niguru* 'to run away.'

There are certain verbal preterits which have present tense meanings. They are those which are passive in form but active in (19 meaning; e.g., *cocoroieta* 'to understand,' *qicoieta* 'to hear,' *voboieta* 'to remember,' *qiqiieta* 'to understand,' *zonjita* 'to know,' and there may be many others. The verbs which follow belong to the first conjugation even though their roots do not end as previously stated.[73] If the present tense of these forms does not change the *i* to *uru* they are exceptional; e.g., *abi,uru* 'to wash oneself,' *fotobi,uru* 'to become soft,' *focorobi,uru* 'to become unstitched,' *cabi* [*cabi,uru*] 'to be moldy,'[74] *sabi* [*sabi,uru*] 'to rust,' *deqi* [*deqi,uru*] 'to be finished, or ended,' *cuchi:cutçuru* 'to rot,' *michi:mitçuru* 'to be filled in by the sea,' *ini,uru* 'to leave,' *nobi:nobiru* or *noburu* 'to be spread out,' *tçuqi,uru* 'to be used,' *vori:uru* 'to descend from above,' *xij:xijru*[75] 'to invite to dine, by compulsion,' *ni:niru* 'to resemble,' *mochij:mochiiuru* 'to evaluate,' *ni:niru* 'to cook,' *mi:miru* 'to look at,' *cori,uru* 'to correct,' *vochi:votçuru* 'to fall,' *i:iru* 'to exist, or be present,' *fugui,uru* 'to pass, as time passes,' *vabi,uru* 'to beg for mercy,' *carabi,uru* 'to become dry,' *iqi:iquru* 'to live,' *fi:firu* 'to become dry,' *qi:quru* 'to come,' *qi:qiru* 'to dress oneself,' *voqi,uru* 'to get out of bed.' The following four verbs have irregular, as well as regular, present tenses;[76] *ataie* has *atóru* 'to give,' *vaqimaie* has *vaqimŏru* 'to discriminate,' *tonaie* has *tonóru* 'to bless,' *sonaie* has *sonóru* 'to place in a high position.'

### *The Preterit, Perfect, Imperfect, and Pluperfect*

In Japanese there is no imperfect. In its place the perfect is used. The perfect is formed in two ways. The first is by suffixing *ta* to the root of a verb ; e.g., *agueta* is the preterit of the verb *ague,uru* 'to offer.' The second is by suffixing *te* to the root and to that adding *gozari,u* or *ari,u* which is then conjugated in the present or the preterit of the second conjugation; e.g., *aguete gozaru* or *aguete gozatta*, or *aguete aru* or *aguete atta* 'offered, or had offered.' If the particle *fáia* [*faia*] is placed before the verb the expression is strengthened; e.g., (20 *fáia aguete gozatta* [*faia* ...] 'I had already offered it.' When the verb *ari,u* is suffixed to the perfect it is not as elegant a way of speaking as when *gozari,u* is used. Therefore when speaking one must be careful about what one says, or in front of whom one speaks, so as to give each person the honor he deserves.

### *The Future of the First Conjugation*

If the root of the verb ends in *te* this syllable is changed to *teô* or *chô* to form the future; e.g., *tate,uru* will become *tateô* or *tachô* 'I shall build.'[77] If the root ends in *ji* the future is formed by changing *ji* to *jô;* e.g., *xenji* becomes *xenjô* 'I shall prepare, or brew, the medicine.' If the root ends in *xe* [*xi*] it changes to *xô*; e.g., *xi* becomes *xô*, and *maraxi* becomes *maraxô* 'I shall do.' If it ends in *ie* it is changed to *io* [*iô*]; e.g., *voxiie* becomes *voxiio* [*vaxiiô*] 'I shall teach.' The remaining roots ending in *e* suffix the particles *ô*, *ôzu*, or *ôzuru*; e.g., *agueô*, *agueôzu*, or *agueôzuru* 'I shall offer.' These endings are used for the first conjugation[78] even when the roots end in *i*; e.g., *deqiôzu* 'I shall be finished.'

The future is also formed by taking the syllable *nu* from the negative present (see below) and putting in its place the particle *baia*. Thus, by taking *nu* away from *aguenu* and putting in its place *baia*, we obtain *aguebaia* 'I will offer.' For *minu* if you take away the *nu* and put in its place *baia* it will become *mibaia* 'I will see, or behold.'

The future perfect is formed by suffixing the particles *te arózu* or *tarózu* to the root; e.g., *aguete arózu* or *aguetarózu* 'I shall already have offered.' The same results are obtained if *faia* is placed before the simple future; e.g., *faia agueôzu*.

(21

### *The Imperative of the First Conjugation*

The imperative of the first conjugation is formed with the root of the verb alone, or with the addition of the particle *io*; e.g., *ague* or *ague io* 'offer!'[79] The future of the imperative is the future absolute *agueô* or *agueôzu*. This is a more elegant and polite way of speaking than giving a command with the regular imperative. The imperative is also formed by taking the *nu* from the negative present (see below) and putting in its place the particle *sai*. Thus, if one takes the *nu* from *aguenu* and replaces it with *sai* it becomes *ague sai* which means 'offer!' If the particle *tai* is placed after the root there is formed a kind of future or optative by which the wish of the speaker is expressed. It is therefore an elegant imperative; thus *mizzu fitotçu nomitai* 'I would like to have a drink of water' is the same as 'give me some water to drink.' When a relative [clause] concerns a precept, rule, admonition, or prohibition the imperative is expressed word for word in whatever the conjugation, affirmative or negative; e.g., *Christiani naru na to no xógun no fatto ga aru* [*Christian ni* ...] 'it is the law of the Shōgan (*imperator*) that no one should become a Christian,' *Padre core vo coxiraie io to voxerareta niiotte* [... *vôxerareta* ...] 'because the Priest told me to do it.'

### *The Optative of the First Conjugation*

The optative, both present and future, is the present tense of the imperative with the particles *negavacu va* or *avare* placed before it and the particles *gana* or *caxi* placed after it. Sometimes it is formed by adding the particle *gana* without any prefix; e.g., *negavacu va ague io caxi?* or *avare aguei gana*[80] 'would that you were to offer?' *avare icanaru tengu, bangue mono nari tomo vare vo totte, fiie no iama ni noboxe io caxi!* (15v)[81] 'Oh! if there were some one, either devil or soothsayer, who could make me ascend the mountain called Hie.' The particle *gana* when it is placed after a noun indicates a wish for the thing specified by the noun; e.g., *saqe gana* 'oh! sake'; and if (22 one is asked if he would like something to drink, the answer is *nani gana* 'would that I had some.'

The perfect of the optative is the second form of the future followed by the particle *mono vo!*; e.g., *niqueozu mono vo!* [*niqueôzu* ...] 'would that I had fled!' The same is achieved by *niguetaraba iocaró mono vo.* Sometimes they say only *niguetaró va* or *niguete aró ni va iocaró mono vo.*

### *The Subjunctive of the First Affirmative Conjugation*

The present tense of the subjunctive is formed by changing the *u* in which the present indicative ends to *eba*; e.g., *aguru* becomes *agureba* 'since I offer.' It is also formed from the present by adding *ni*, *de*, *vo*, or *va* to the particle *tocoro* according to the case requirements of the verb that follows, with the first verb being controlled by the noun; e.g., *aru toqi Pedro chinsui xite iraruru tocoro ie fito ga qite* (16v)[82] 'since a certain man came to the place where Peter was when he was drunk,' *nhóbó ni tachi vacarete iru tocoro ni* (16v)[83] 'since they were separated and divorced,' *có aru tocoro ni* 'since things are this way,' *ioso ie zzuru tocoro va fito ni corosareta* (16v)[84] 'when he went outside, he was killed by someone,' *go misa vo asobaruru tocoro vo uchi coroita* (121)[85] 'he killed him while he was celebrating mass.' This is a general rule which applies to all conjugations.

The perfect and the pluperfect of the subjunctive are formed from these same tenses in the indicative with the addition of the particle *reba*; e.g., *agueta reba* 'since he had offered.' It is also formed by taking away *gozaru* from the preterit pluperfect and putting in its place *atta reba* or *atta*; but, when *atta* is used, the particles *ni, vo, va,* or *ie* must be added according to the requirements of the following verb, just as with *tocoro* in the present tenses; e.g., *aguete atta reba* or *aguete atta ni, vo, va,* or *ie* 'since I had already offered it.'

The future of the subjunctive is formed by adding the particle *toqi* to the future indicative; e.g., *agueô toqi* 'since he would offer it later.'

The pluperfect subjunctive, with all the expressions (*vox*) which signify that which comes after a completed action, is formed by (23 placing *cara, nochi,* or *igo* after the pluperfect indicative, minus *gozaru*; e.g., *aguete cara, nochi,* or *igo, mairó* 'I shall leave after he has offered it.' This is like *aguetaró toki mairó* 'I shall leave after he has already offered it.' *Agueôzuru ni* or *agueôzuru tocoro ni* means 'since he was already prepared to offer it.' *Agueôzuru coto no saqi ni* means 'a little while before he offered it.'

The present tense of the permissive subjunctive is formed in two ways. The first is by changing the *u* of the present indicative to *edomo*; e.g., *aguredomo* 'although I could offer it.'

The preterit of the permissive subjunctive is formed by adding *redomo* to the preterit indicative; e.g., *agueta redomo* 'although he had offered it.' The future permissive is formed by adding *redomo* to the second form of the future indicative; e.g., *agueôzu redomo* 'although he would be able to offer it.' The second form of the permissive subjunctive is formed by adding the particle *tomo* to the present indicative; e.g., *aguru tomo* 'although he could offer it.' The particles *mamaio* or *madeio* may also be added to the present tense; e.g., *sore vo voxiiuru mamaio* or *sore vo voxiiuru madeio* 'although he could teach this.'

The preterit of the second permissive is formed by suffixing *ritomo* to the preterit indicative; e.g., *agueta ritomo* 'although he had offered it.' The same meaning is achieved by adding the particles *mamaio* or *madeio* to the preterit indicative; e.g., *agueta mamaio* or *agueta madeio*; or by adding *tote* to the preterit subjunctive; e.g., *aguetareba tote.*

The future permissive is formed by adding *tomo* to the second form of the future indicative; e.g., *agueozu tomo* [*agueôzu tomo* 'although he would offer it']. It is also formed by adding *mamaio* or *madeio* to the same future form. If the particle *tatoi* is placed before the forms of the permissive subjunctive great strength is added to the sentence; e.g., *tatoi vôxeraruru tomo* 'even though you may state this.' The same meaning is obtained by removing the verbs *gozaru* or *aru* from the pluperfect indicative and replacing it with the particle *mo*; e.g., *aguete mo* 'although he may offer it.' The same *mo* when placed after the present indicative gives the same meaning; e.g., *doco de qiqi marasuru mo, sono sata va mósanu* 'although he hears that everywhere, he does not pay any attention.' The same meaning is obtained by the sentences *ague mo xeio caxi?, aguete mo xô madeio,* and *nanto mo ague caxi?* [... *aguei caxi?*][86] 'although he offers.' *Aguru ni saxerarei,* (24 *agueta ni saxerarei,* or *agueo ni saxerarei* [*agueô* ...] have the meanings of 'although he could have offered, although he could offer, or although he would offer'; or one might say 'let us offer' or 'let us give.'

## *The Infinitive*

The present infinitive is formed by adding *coto* or *to* to the present indicative; e.g., *aguru coto* or *aguru to* 'to offer.'

The preterit infinitive is formed by adding the same particles to the preterit indicative; e.g., *agueta coto* or *agueta to* 'to have offered.' The future infinitive is formed by adding the same particles to the future indicative; e.g., *agueô coto* or *agueô to* 'to be about to offer.' The same meaning is obtained by adding *ióni* to the present, preterit, or future indicative; e.g., *nai nai guioi ni caqerareô ióni va vare mo zonzuru fitobito mo zonjita* (22v) 'I think and others believed me to have been favored by you with many benefits,' *qeccu vare ni voxiie marasuru ióni gozaru* (117v) 'he is truly able to teach me,' *agueta ióni gozaru* 'he is said to have offered it.'

To ask or answer a question the infinitive is often subordinate to the verb which follows; e.g., *nhóbógata ni vochita coto ga atta ca?* 'did you fall into the sin of adultery with this woman? is this what happened?' etc. All the tenses of the infinitive are used in the same way.

Sometimes the preterit infinitive is replaced by the pluperfect with *gozaru* or *aru* removed; e.g., *Deus no minori vo firomete iocaró* 'it is good to spread the Gospel.' Sometimes the present or preterit indicative plus *ga* replaces the present or preterit of the infinitive; e.g., *sore vo vôxeraruru ga varú gozaró* 'it will be bad to say that,' *maitta ga maxi gia* (21) 'it is better to have come, or it was better to come.'

When the substantive verb follows the infinitive, the particle *coto* is not required; e.g., *cosacazzuqi de va saqe vo nomu devanai* (23) 'to drink sake from a small glass is not to drink sake,' *core coso caqu de gozare* 'this we are able to say, or better, write,' *caqu de gozatte coso* 'this is not the way for it to be written,' *sore va aguru devanai* 'that is not to offer it.' Some of these examples are taken from other (25 conjugations but the general rule applies to all. The idea of the infinitive is also obtained by the following means of expression; *ague va, aguredomo* 'although I offered, or even if I made it so that it was offered.' Because this is a general rule for all the conjugations, they also say *qiqi va tçucamatçure domo gatten xenu* 'although I have listened, or done everything necessary to hear; I still don't understand.' They also say *aguru vo motte* 'by offering, or with the fact that he is to offer,' *aguru iori* 'from the fact that he is to offer,' *aguru nitçuite* 'about the fact that he is to offer.'

The gerund in *Di* is the present or future indicative followed by the particle *jibun*, or less frequently some other particle meaning 'time'; e.g., *aguru jibun* 'the time for offering,' *agueô ni qivamatta* 'he made the decision that it be offered,' *niguru jibun gia* 'it is time to flee,' *corosareôzuru ni aisadamatte arŏzu* (13) 'it will have been decided that he will be killed, or will have to be killed.'

The gerund in *Do* is formed in two ways. The first is by adding the particles *ni* or *tote* to the present indicative; e.g., *aguruni* or *agurutote iurusareta* 'I was freed by it being offered.' The second way is by removing the verb *gozaru* from the pluperfect; e.g., *aguete cutabireta* 'I became tired by offering, or raising up,' that is to say, 'from the action of presenting, or raising up, I suffered the result of becoming tired.' There is also another elegant, and frequently used, way to form the gerund in *Do*. It is done by placing the root of the verb in front of another verb making a compound; e.g., *fiqi iosuru* 'to approach, pulling.' The roots which are used in this way do not change with respect to their function. The gerund in *Do* is also used to express purpose *taixó to xite* 'since he was a commander (*dux*), or was fulfilling the function of a commander,' *von rei to xite* 'giving thanks,' *rŏtai nomi ni xite* 'since he was an old man,' *tçucai xite ivaruru* 'he said it as a messenger.'

The gerund in *Dum* is formed by adding the particles *tame* or *tote* to the present or future indicative; e.g., *aguru tame* or *agueo tote* [*agueô tote*] 'in order to offer.' The same meaning is obtained by *aguru ni fatto ga aru* 'there is a law about offering,' unless this should be considered a gerund in ni [*Di*].

The supine in *Tum* is formed in two ways. The first is by adding *ni* to the root. The second is by adding *tameni* to the present indicative; e.g., *tazzune ni maitta* or *tazzunuru tameni maitta* 'I came in order to obtain it.'

The supine in *Tu* is the root of the verb alone. To obtain the same meaning they also use *mósu ni voiobanu* 'it is not necessary to (26 speak.'

The present, preterit, and future participles are formed by adding the particles *fito* or *mono* to the indicative. When *fito* is used the result is a more honorable way of speaking; e.g., *aguru fito* or *aguru mono* 'he who offers,' *agueta fito* 'he who offered,' *agueô mono* 'he who will offer,' *Buppôgacu suru tomogara ni voite va* (73v) 'as for those who devote themselves to the study of the laws of idolatry,' *von vo xiru vo fito to va iúzo; von vo xiranu voba chicuxó to coso iie* (96v). In this last sentence the *vo* takes the place of the participle, and the sentence therefore means 'those who know kindness (*beneficia*) are correctly called men; those who do not know it are truly called beasts.' This is a general rule for all the conjugations and therefore the example contains a verb from the second conjugation. The participle is also made by adding *te* ['hand'] to the root of the verb; e.g., *aguete* 'one who offers.'

### *The First Negative Conjugation*

The negative root is formed by adding *zu* to the affirmative root; e.g., *aguezu*.

The present tense is formed with *nu* instead of *zu*; e.g., *aguenu* 'I do not offer.' This is a general rule no matter how the root ends. The only exceptions are *xi* and *maraxi* which form the negative present in *xenu* and *maraxenu* 'I do not do.' The roots that end in *ji* change the *ji* to *je* and then suffix the particle *nu* to the present; e.g., *zonji* in the negative present becomes *zonienu* [*zonjenu*] 'I do not know.' In some areas of Japan they form the negative by removing the final *u* from the negative root and adding *ari,u*, which is then conjugated according to the required tense; e.g., *aguezaru* 'I do not offer,' *aguezatta* 'I did not offer,' *aguezatta reba* 'since I did not offer.' They also say *aguezu xite* 'by not offering.'[87]

The negative of the preterit is formed in like manner by adding the particle *nanda* instead of *nu*; e.g., *aguenanda* 'I did not offer,' *zonjenanda* 'I did not know,' *vorinanda* 'I did not descend.'

The pluperfect is formed by changing the last *a* of the preterit to *e* and adding the verb *gozaru* in the present and *gozatta* in the preterit; e.g., *aguenande gozaru* or *aguenande gozatta* 'I have not offered.' It is also formed by adding *ide gozaru* or *ide gozatta* instead of (27 *nande gozaru*; e.g., *agueide gozaru* or *agueide gozatta* 'I had not offered,' *zonzeide gozaru* [*zonjeide* ... ][88] 'I had not known,' *vochiide gozatta* 'I had not fallen.'

The negative future is formed by adding *mai* or *maji* to the affirmative root or the affirmative present tense; e.g., *ague mai* or *aguru maji* 'you will not offer.'

The imperative is formed by placing *na* after the present indicative; *aguru na* 'do not offer.'

It is also formed by placing *na* before the root and *so* after it; e.g., *na ague so* 'do not offer.'

It is also formed by placing *na* after the root; e.g., *ague na* 'do not offer,' *mixe na* 'do not show,' *mesare na* 'do not do.' The roots which end in *xi* or *ji*, but are in the first conjugation,[89] change the *i* to *e* to form the negative imperative; e.g., *sǒ xe na* or *só maraxe na* 'do not do that,' *sǒ zonze na* [*só zonje na*] 'do not think that.'

The optative is formed by placing *negavacuva* or *avare* before the negative imperative and placing *caxi* or *gana* after it; e.g., *avare aguru na caxi* 'oh! if only you would not offer,' and *negavacuva na ague so gana* with the same meaning.

The preterit of the optative is formed by placing *mono vo* after the negative future; e.g., *aguru mai mono vo* 'oh! if only you would not have offered.'

The negative subjunctive is formed by changing the *u* which ends the negative present to *eba*; e.g., *agueneba* 'since he did not offer.'

The preterit of the subjunctive is formed by adding *reba* to the negative preterit of the indicative; e.g., *aguenanda reba* 'since he had not offered.'

The future of the subjunctive is formed by adding *qereba* to the negative future; e.g., *niguru mai qereba* 'since he is not going to escape.'

The permissive subjunctive is formed by adding *domo* to the negative present after changing the final *u* of the verb to *e*; e.g., *aguenedomo* 'although he cannot offer.' They also say, and this usage is preferred, *aguenaidemo* or *agueidemo* 'even if he not offer.'[90]

The preterit of the permissive subjunctive is formed by placing *redomo* after the negative preterit; e.g., *aguenanda redomo* 'although he had not offered.' *Aguenaidemo* or *agueidemo* 'although he would not be allowed to offer,' is also said.

The permissive future is formed by adding *qeredomo* to the negative future; e.g., *aguru mai qeredomo* 'although he is not going to be allowed to offer.' (28

Another way of forming the permissive subjunctive is to place the particle *tomo* after the negative root; e.g., *aguezu tomo* 'although he is not going to be able to offer.' It is also formed by placing *tote* after the [negative] present subjunctive; e.g., *agueneba tote.* A third way is to add *mamaio* or *madeio* to the negative present; e.g., *aguenu mamaio* or *aguenu madeio* 'although he cannot offer.'

The preterit is formed by placing *ritomo* after the negative preterit; e.g., *aguenanda ritomo* 'although he had not offered.' It is also formed by placing *tote* after the negative preterit of the subjunctive; e.g., *aguenanda reba tote,* or better, *aguenaidemo* or *agueidemo* 'although he does not offer, or had not offered.'

The future is formed by placing *tomo* after the negative future; e.g., *aguemai tomo* 'although he is not going to offer,' *vochiidemo* 'although he will not fall.'

The present, preterit, and future infinitives are the present, preterit, and future negative indicative present tenses followed by *coto* or *to*; e.g., *aguenu coto* 'not to offer,' *aguenanda coto* 'not to have offered,' *aguru mai coto* 'not to be going to offer.'

Sometimes they use the negative present instead of the preterit in all the conjugations; e.g., *mi maraxenu* 'I did not see.'

The negative gerund in *Di* is the same as the negative present or future; e.g., *aguenu* or *aguru mai* 'of not offering.'

The gerund in *Do* is formed by placing *ni* after the negative root or the negative present tense; e.g., *aguezuni* or *aguenuni* 'by not offering.' The same meaning is obtained with *agueide, aguenaide* or *aguezu xite.*

The gerund in *Dum* is formed by placing *tote* or *tame* after the [negative] present or future of the indicative; e.g., *aguenu tame* or *aguru mai tote* 'in order not to offer.'

The present, preterit, and future participles are formed by adding *fito* or *mono* to the negative of the present, preterit, and future indicatives; e.g., *aguenu fito* 'he who is not offering,' *aguenanda mono* 'he who did not offer,' *aguru mai mono* 'he who will not offer,' *aguenaide cara* or *agueide nochi* 'after he had not offered, after they did not offer, or after it was not offered.'

(29

*The Second Affirmative Conjugation*

All the roots of the second conjugation end in *i* and form their present tense by changing *i* to *u*; e.g., *iomi:iomu* 'I read.' If the root ends in *chi* it changes its ending to *tçu* e.g., *machi:matçu* 'I wait.' If the root ends in *xi* it changes to *su*; e.g., *coroxi:corosu* 'I kill.'

For the preterit, if the root ends in *ami* it changes to *óda*; e.g., *cami:códa* 'I ate, or chewed.' If it ends in *ebi* or *emi* it changes to *eôda*; e.g., *saqebi:saqeôda* 'I am injured,' *sonemi:soneoda* [*soneôda*] 'I envied, or I had envy.' If it ends in *obi* or *omi* it changes to *ôda*; e.g., *corobi:corôda* 'he fell,' *comi:côda* 'it enclosed itself.' If it ends in *umi* it changes to *únda* [*unda*]; e.g., *casumi:casunda* 'it is cloudy.' The same change is made for roots ending in *imi*; e.g., *canaximi:canaxúnda* [*canaxunda*] 'he became sad.' If it ends in *gui* it changes to *ida*; e.g., *fegui:feida* 'it is divided.' *Xini,uru* has the preterit *xinda* 'he is dead,' and *ini:uru* has the preterit *inda* 'he left.' While in this respect they [*xini* and *ini*] are in the second conjugation, in the other tenses they are in the first. A root ending in *chi* or *ri* changes in the preterit to *tta*; e.g., *mochi:motçu* in the preterit becomes *motta* 'he received,' *chiri,u:chitta* 'it is scattered.' Those which end in *xi* or *qi* change to *ita*; e.g., *coroxi,u:coroita* 'he killed,' *qiqi,u:qiita* 'he heard,' *xiqi,u:xiita* 'he stretched it out.'

The future is formed by changing the *i* in which the root ends to *ó, ŏzu, ózuru*; e.g., *iomó, iomŏzu,* or *iomózuru* 'you will read.' If the root ends in *chi* it changes to *tó*; e.g., *machi:mató* 'I shall wait.' A root ending in *xi* changes to *só*; e.g., *móxi,u:mósó* 'I shall say, or speak.'

The imperative is formed by changing the *i* in which the root ends to *e*; e.g., *iomi:iome* 'read! or may you read.' If the root ends in *chi* it changes to *te*; e.g., *machi:mate* 'wait!' The imperative is also formed by changing the *nu* in which the negative present ends to *ai*; if you remove the *nu* from *iomanu* and replace it with *ai* it gives you *yomai* 'read!'[91] This is a common rule for the third conjugation, but this imperative is used only when addressing inferiors.

The future of the imperative is the future absolute; e.g., (30 *iomó* 'you will read.' This is used when addressing very low people.

The remaining tenses of the optative, subjunctive, gerund, and infinitive are formed in the same way and with the same particles as are used for each in the first conjugation.

### *The Second Negative Conjugation*

The root of the negative second conjugation is made by changing *i*, in which the affirmative root ends, to *azu*; e.g., *iomi:iomazu* 'not reading.'

If the root ends in *chi* the present tense is formed by changing it to *tanu*; e.g., *machi:matanu* 'I do not wait.' If it ends in *xi* it changes to *sanu*; e.g., *coroxi:corosanu* 'I do not kill.' If they end in any other way change *i* to *anu*; e.g., *corobi:corobanu* 'I do not fall.'

The preterit is formed by changing the *nu* of the present tense to *nanda*; e.g., *corobanu:corobananda* 'I did not fall,' *iomananda* 'I did not read.' The other tenses are formed in the same way as the negative first conjugation.

### *The Third Affirmative Conjugation*

The roots of the third conjugation end in *ai*, *oi*, or *ui*. Those ending in *ai* change to *ó* to form the present; e.g., *narai:naró* 'I learn.' Those ending in *oi* change to *ô*; e.g., *vomoi:vomô* 'I think.' Those ending in *ui* change to *ú*; e.g., *cui:cú* 'I eat.'

The preterit is formed by adding *ta* to the present tense; e.g., *naróta* 'I learned,' *vomôta* 'I thought,' *cúta* 'I ate.'

The pluperfect is formed by changing the final *a* of the preterit to *e* and adding the verb *gozaru* in the present and *gozatta* in the past, in the same way as we have described for the first conjugation; e.g., *naróte gozaru* or *narŏte gozatta* 'I have already learned.'

The future is formed by changing the final *i* of the root to *vó*, *vózu*, or *vózuru*; e.g., *naravó*, *naravŏzu*, or *naravózuru* 'I shall learn.' If the root ends in *oi* it is changed to *vô*, *vôzu*, or *vôzuru* [*vŏ*, *vŏzu*, (31 or *vŏzuru*]; e.g., *vomoi:vomouô*, *vomovozu*, or *vomovôzuru* [*vomoi:vomovŏ*, *vomovŏzu*, or *vomovŏzuru*] 'I shall think.'[92]

The imperative is formed by placing *e* after the root; e.g., *naraie* 'learn!' *toie* 'ask!' *cuie* 'eat!'[93] It is also formed by removing the syllable *nu* from the negative present tense and replacing it with the letter *i*; e.g., *naravai* 'learn!' *tovai* 'ask!' *cuvai* 'eat!' This form is used when addressing inferiors, as are those of the other conjugations.

### *The Third Negative Conjugation*

The root of the third negative conjugation is formed by changing the *i* of the affirmative root to *vazu*; e.g., *naravazu*, *tovazu*, and *cuvazu*. The present tense is formed by changing the *i* to *vanu*; e.g., *naravanu* 'I do not learn,' *tovanu* 'I do not ask,' *cuvanu* 'I do not eat.'

The preterit is formed by changing the *i* of the root to *vananda*; e.g., *naravananda* 'I did not learn,' *tovananda* 'I did not ask,' *cuvananda* 'I did not eat.'

The pluperfect is formed by changing the final *a* of the preterit to *e* and adding the verb *gozaru* or *gozatta*; e.g., *cuvanande gozatta* 'I had not eaten,' or *naravanande gozaru* 'I had not learned.' The remaining forms are like the other conjugations.[94]

If the substantive verb is placed after the gerund in *Do* for all the affirmative and negative conjugations, it means that the action signified by the gerund is or is not done; e.g., *aguete aró* 'it will already be offered,' *cono qió ga caite gozaranu* 'this book is not written,' *agueide arózu* 'he will not yet have offered.' The substantive verbs are *gozaru:gozaranu*, *voru:vori nai*, *dea* or *gia:devanai*, *aru:aranu* or *gozaranu*, *voru:voranu*, and each of these verbs follows the general rules for its conjugation.[95]

If the substantive verb from any of the conjugations is placed after the infinitive form it means that whatever is signified by the infinitive is, was, or will be; or the negative thereof; e.g., *aguru coto aró* 'it will be that he offers,' that is to say 'he will offer,' *naróta coto gozaru mai* 'he will not learn.' All these substantive verbs are conjugated in the second conjugation to which they belong by virtue of the fact that their (32 roots end in *i*; *ari,u:gozari,u*.

*The Conjugation of the Negative Substantive Verb*

The negative substantive verb is *nai, gozanai,* or *vori nai* which means 'not to be.' Its root is *naqu, gozanaqu,* or *vori naqu.*

The preterit is formed by changing the *i* in which the present tense ends to *c* and then adding the preterit of *ari,u* which is *atta*; e.g., *nacatta* or *gozanacatta* 'he was not.' The other tenses are conjugated, as is *ari,u,* in the second conjugation.

The imperative is *nacare, nanaiso,* or *nai na* 'be not!'

The subjunctive is formed by changing the *i* of the present tense to *qereba*; e.g., *naqereba* or *gozanaqereba* 'if it be not.'

The permissive subjunctive is formed by changing the *i* of the present to *qeredomo*; e.g., *gozanaqeredomo* 'although he is not.'

The preterit of the subjunctive is formed by adding *redomo* to the preterit of the indicative; e.g., *nacatta redomo* 'although he was not.'

The substantive [verb] with the particle *tomo* is formed with the root; e.g., *naqu tomo* 'even if it were not.' The gerund is *nó, nóte, naqu xite,* or *nacatte* 'since it is not.' The remaining are formed as above, with the verb *ari,u* added, and are conjugated in the second conjugation.

Adjectives, when they do not precede verbs, are conjugated in the same way as the negative substantive verb. The adjectives, which have been said above to end in *ai, ei, oi, ui,* and *ij,* form their roots by changing the final *i* to *qu*; e.g., *fucaqu* is the root of 'deep,' *ioqu* the root of 'good,' *xiguequ* the root of 'dense,' *varuqu* the root of 'bad,' and *vonajiqu* the root of 'the same.'

The present tense is the form (*vox*) of the adjective itself; e.g., *ioi* 'good,' *fucai* 'deep,' *varui* 'bad,' *vonaji* 'the same.'[96]

The preterit is formed by changing the *i* of the adjective to *c* or *q* and adding *ari,u*. This form is then conjugated according to (33 the tense required by the sentence.

The permissive subjunctive with *tomo* is *fucaqu tomo* or *fucai tomo* 'although deep.'

The gerund in *Do* is *fucóte* 'since it was deep,' *ióte* 'since it was good,' *canaxiúte* [*canaxúte*][97] 'since it was sad,' *xingueote* [*xigeôte*][98] 'since it was dense.' It also takes the form of *fucó xite*, *fucaqu xite*, or *fucacatte*, or again *iô xite*, *ioqu xite*, or *iocatte*.

The adjectives which end in *na* are not conjugated. There is, however, a gerund in *Do*. For example, *aqiracana* has for its gerund *aqiracani xite* 'since it was clear,' and with the same meaning there is *aqiraca de*. *Arisóna* has *arisŏni xite* 'since it became apparent, or easy to believe.' *Ióna* has *ióni* as in *ióni xite* 'since it is in a good way, or since it has a good manner.' *Cava ga fucóte vatarananda* 'because the river was deep, I did not cross it,' *xebŏte irarenu* 'since it was narrow, he was unable to enter,' *varúte cuvarenu* 'it is inedible, or it cannot be eaten, because it is bad.' The other tenses of the adjective, as has been said, are formed with the verb *ari,u* and conjugated according to the requirements of the sentence. The negative conjugation is also formed with *ari,u*; e.g., if the root is *fucacarazu* the present tense is *fucacaranu* 'it is not deep.' The preterit is *fucacarananda* 'it was not, etc.'

### *The Conditional Particles*[99]

There are five particles which make an utterance (*oratio*) conditional; *naraba*, *ni voite va*, *raba*, *va*, and *ba*. When the first two are placed after any verb, affirmative or negative, present, preterit, or future, the result is that the verb becomes conditional. For example; *niguru naraba* 'if you flee,' *iôda ni voite va* 'if you had read,' *naravó naraba* 'if you will learn,' *cuvazu ni voite va*[100] 'if you do not eat.' Sometimes *voi* [*voite*] is removed from *ni voite va*; *agueô ni va* 'if you would offer,' *aguetaró ni va* 'if you would have offered.' Sometimes *voite* [*voite va*] is removed, leaving only *ni*; e.g., *mairó ni coso, nen goro ni mŏsŏzure* (19) 'if I go, or if I shall have gone, I will tell him so in a friendly way,' *xitaró ni coso, saisocu tçuqu maji qere* (19) 'if I (34 had done it, it would not have been done with diligence and persuasion.'

The particle *raba* is placed after the preterit;[101] e.g., *naróta raba* 'if I would have learned,' *naravananda raba* 'if I would not have learned.'

The particle *va* is added to the negative roots of all three conjugations; e.g., *aguezu va* 'if I not offer,' *iomazu va* 'if I not read,' *naravazu va* 'if I not learn,' *naqu va* 'if it not be,' *fucacarazu va* 'if it be not deep.'

The particle *ba* has the same effect and is, like *va*, joined to the root; *aguezũba, iomazũba, naravazũba*.[102] If the particle *ba* replaces the negative *zu*, an affirmative conditional is formed; e.g., *agueba*, 'if I offer,' *iomaba* 'if I read,' *naravaba* 'if I learn,' and *iocaraba* 'if it be good.' The particle *va* is not only added to the negative roots of adjectives, but also to the affirmative; e.g., *fucaqu va* 'if it be deep,' *vonajiqu va* 'if it be the same.' Sometimes they use this expression to give the idea 'if it be not too troublesome, will you do it.' They also say *aguemajiqu va* 'if you would not offer.'

The particle *ni voite va* is joined to nouns in such a way as to substitute for the substantive verb; e.g., *jójó ni voite va uqe toró* (121v)[103] 'I shall get it, if it be very good, or the best,' *curuxicarazaru gui ni voite va* 'if it would not have been unpleasant, or if it had not been an unpleasant thing.'

If the particle *saie* is placed in a clause (*oratio*) in which there is already a conditional particle, it adds strength to the meaning; e.g., *fune saie mairu naraba* 'if only a ship were to come,' *sonata saie vocutabire naku va* (118) 'if he be not tired,' or it might be said 'as for me, or as far as it depends upon me, I am not tired.'

The particle *saie* alone sometimes forms a conditional; e.g., *Niffon no xôcocu ni saie caióna coto gozaru fodo ni* [*Nifon* ...] (118) 'if in the small kingdom of Japan things of this kind be found, or exist,' that is to say 'how much more there will be in a large one,' *coco moto no tocai ni saie meivacu itasu ióni gozaru fodoni, etc.* (118) 'on the voyage here I suffered very much, and so ...,' *fito saie côquai suru mono vo iurusu ni ivan ia, Deus ni voite voia?* [... *va?*] (118v) 'if one forgives one who repents, how much more will God,' *core fodo xei vo iruru saie coto naricanuru ni; ucato xite va, incadeca banji canavŏzo?* [... *icadeca* ...] (119) 'if gathering all one's strength this can be done only with difficulty, how could it be done if it were done without any strength?,' *core saie xinicui ni* 'if this be difficult to do,' *fune de saie ioio tçuita* (35 *ni, cachi va nananaca naru mai* [... *nacanaca naru mai*] (119v) 'if I arrived by ship with such difficulties, without doubt I could not have done it on foot.'

### *The Potential Verb*[104]

The placing of the particle rŏ[105] after the present or future tense makes a potential; e.g., *aguru rŏ* 'he perhaps offers,' *nigueozurŏ* [*nigueôzurŏ*] 'he will perhaps escape.'

The preterit is made by changing *ta* to *tçu* and adding rŏ; e.g., *aguetçurŏ* 'he perhaps offered.' But if it is added to the negative preterit, the *da* must be changed to *zzu*; e.g., *aguenanzzurŏ* 'it has perhaps not been offered, etc.'

The present potential is also formed by adding *arŏzu* [*mo arŏzu*] or other future verbs to the infinitive; e.g., *aguru coto mo arŏzu* or *ague mo xôzu* 'he will perhaps offer.'

The preterit is formed by adding this same future to the preterit infinitive; e.g., *agueta coto mo arŏzu* 'he perhaps offered.'

The future is *agueô coto mo arŏzu* 'he will perhaps offer.' The negative is formed in the same way; e.g., *aguenu, aguenanda*, or *aguru mai coto mo arŏzu* 'he perhaps does not offer, he perhaps did not offer, or he will perhaps not offer.' When we wish to say that something is perhaps the case we use *mono* instead of *coto*; e.g., *noxenanda mono de arózu* 'they perhaps did not place it aboard ship,' *iqi chigŏta mono de arŏzu* 'they seem not to have met along the way,' *moreqicoieta mono de gozarŏ ca to zonzuru* 'I believe it is perhaps as it has been said.'

To express the meaning 'become' the verb *nari,u* is added to the adjective and then conjugated according to the requirements of the adjective taken adverbally; e.g., *fucŏ naru* 'it becomes deep,' *varŭ natta* 'it became bad.' Also they say *fucŏ aru* 'it is deep,' and sometimes *fucŏ nai* 'it is not deep.' They obtain this same meaning by conjugating *nai* according to the tense required by the sentence. They also use *fucŏ nai coto mo arŏzu* 'perhaps it will be that this is not deep.' (36

### *The Conjugation of Irregular Verbs*[106]

The verb *qi,uru* 'to come' has *quru* 'I come,' *qita* 'I came,' *côzu* 'I shall come,' *coi* or *coio* 'come!' *qitareba* 'since he will have come, or would have come,' *qitaredomo* 'although he came.' The negative root is *côzu* [*cozu*] and the negative present is *conu* 'I do not come.' *Mede*, which is the root of the verb meaning 'to enjoy,' has a present in *mezzuru* and its gerund in *Do* is *medete* 'by enjoying.' *Cui*, which is the root of the verb meaning 'to be mournful,' has its present in *cuiuru*. Its gerund in *Do* is *cuite* 'by mourning,' its negative root is *cuizu*, and its negative present is *cuinu*. *Araie*, which is the root of the verb 'to be,'[107] has a present in *araiuru* or *arŏru* 'it is.' *Furi*, which is the root of the verb 'to become old,' has a preterit in *furita* 'he became old,' and a gerund in *Do* which is *furite* 'by becoming old.' *Fe*, the root of the verb meaning 'to cross over,' has a present in *furu* 'he crosses over,' and a preterit in *feta* 'he crossed over.' *Tari,u* is a verb which signifies that a thing is complete or entire. It has a present in *taru* 'it is complete,' a preterit in *tatta* 'it was complete,' and a future in *tari maraxo* [*maraxô*] 'it will be complete.' Its negative root is *tarazu*, its negative present is *taranu*, its preterit is *tarananda* 'it was not complete,' its future is *taru mai* 'it will not be complete,' and its imperfect subjunctive is *taraneba* 'since it has not been completed.'

The [negative] permissive is *taranedomo*, the infinitive is *taranu coto*, and the gerund in *Do* is *taraide* or *tarazu xite*. The verb *taxi:tasu*, which means 'to complete, or finish,' has a future in *taxi maraxô* 'I shall finish.' *Tasanu* is the negative present. *Tari* [*Tarai*] is the root of the verb *tarŏ* which has the meaning 'to be completed.' In the negative the preterit is *taravananda* 'it was not completed,' the subjunctive is *taravaneba* 'since it is not completed,' the permissive is *taravanedomo*, the infinitive is *taravanu coto*, and the gerund in *Do* is *taravaide* or *taravaxu xite* [*taravazu xite*]. *Vocotari* is the root of the verb *vocotaru* 'to be negligent.' It has an infinitive in *vocotaru coto*, a negative root in *vocotarazu*, and a negative present in *voicotaranu* [*vocotaranu*]. *Voi* is the root of a verb which has a preterit in *voita* 'he was old.' (37 *Voitaru* has the same meaning. The negative present is *voinu* and the gerund in *Do* is *voite*. *Urei* is the root of the verb 'to be sad.' It has a present in *ureô*, an imperative in *ure io* [*ureie io*][108] an infinitive in *ureoru coto* [*ureôru* ...].[109] Its gerund in *Do* is *ureite*. *Tomi* is the root of the verb *tomu* or *tomeru* 'to become rich.' Its preterit is *tonda*, its gerund in

*Do* is *tonde*, and its negative root is *tomazu*. *Saiguiri,u* means 'to go before, or anticipate.' Its preterit is *saiguitta* and its gerund in *Do* is *saiguitte*.

### *The Aforementioned Verbs—Their Formation and Diversity*[110]

In this language there are simple active, causative active, passive, neutral, and impersonal verbs.[111] All are conjugated by the three conjugations according to the way in which their roots terminate.

From certain adjectives come (*procedo*) certain verbs; e.g., from *catai* 'hard' comes *catame,uru* 'I make hard' which is active, *catamari,u* 'I become hard' which is neutral, *catamerare,uru* 'I am made hard' which is passive. From the adjective *canaxii* 'sad' comes *canaximi,u* which means 'to be sad.'

The causative verbs (*verba faciendi facere*) are formed with the particles *saxe* or *xe*. The first is added to the roots of verbs in the first conjugation, [112] while the second is [not] added to the roots of the second and third conjugation, but rather to the negative present after the *nu* has been removed; e.g., *aguesaxe,uru* 'I make him offer,' *iomaxe,uru* 'I make him read,' *naravaxe,uru* 'I make him learn.' All of these forms are in the first conjugation because the particles end in *e*. Sometimes, but rarely, *saxe* follows verbs of the second and third conjugation, but this is to make the verbs more elegant. It is used with the particle *rare* to honor someone; e.g., *iomasaxe rare,uru* ['he makes him read']. *Padre va dojucu ni cathecismo vo naravasaxeraruru* 'the priest orders his servant to learn his cathecism,'[113] *mono no fon vo fito ni* (38 *iomasaxeraruru* (162v.) 'he makes him read his book.'

The passive verbs (*verba passiva*) are made with the particles *rare* and *re*. The particle *rare* is added to the active verbs, according to the way explained before, after removing the *nu* from the negative form; e.g., *aguerare,uru* 'I am offered it,' *iomare,uru* 'I am read to,' *naravare,uru* 'I am taught.' They use these passive forms to mean 'to be read to by someone,' or 'to be, or not to be legible.' There are other passive forms which come from neutral verbs or verbs which have neutral meanings. They are also formed with the particles *rare* and *re*, but when they are so formed they do not govern the cases common to the passive (for which see below) but rather the cases of the verbs from which they come; e.g., from *agari,u* comes *agarare,uru*; and, since *agari,u* 'I ascend' requires the accusative, this verb also requires the accusative. For example; *cono iama ie agararenu* (102) 'it is not possible to climb this mountain, or this mountain is unable to be climbed,' *xiro cara derarenu* (102) 'it is not possible to leave the castle,' *xebóte irarenu* (102) 'it is not possible to penetrate because it is too narrow, or confined,' *cono michi va arucarenu* (102) 'it is not possible to walk this street,' *natçu va coco ni irare mai* 'it will not be possible to live here during the summer,' *cono fude de va cacarenu* (102) 'it cannot be written with this pen,' *fima ga nóte cacarenanda* (102) 'it cannot be written because of the lack of time,' *cono bun ni coso cacaruru mono de gozare* (69v) 'it will indeed be well written in this way,' *axi ga itóte arucarenu* (102) 'it is impossible to walk because of painful feet.' All of these passive verbs are of the first conjugation.[114] The neutral verbs (*verba neutra*) are those which have a neutral meaning; i.e., being initiated by oneself, and not by others. For example; *ivo ga toruru* 'the fish are caught,' *caje ga toruru* 'the wind ceases,' *ito ga qiruru* 'the string is cut,' *ji ga iomuru* (100) 'the letter [Chinese character] is well read,' *aqi,u* 'I am uncovered.' *Qiri,u* 'I cut' is active, *qirare,uru* is passive, and *qire,uru* 'I am cut' is neutral. This last form is used when a sword cuts well because it is sharp. *Qiraxe,uru* is a causative verb which means 'I make someone cut.' *Ague,uru* means 'I raise,' *aguerare,uru* 'I am raised' passively, *aguesaxe,uru* 'I make someone raise,' *agari,u* 'I am raised' neutrally, *agarare,uru* 'to be ascendable,' *agaraxe,uru* 'I cause something to be raised, or I cause him or it to raise himself or itself.' If to these verbs are added the particles which indicate honor (see below) other combinations are made. The adjectives when they are conjugated have a neutral meaning; e.g., *fidarui* 'I am thirsty,' *fucacatta* 'it was deep.'

The impersonal verbs (*verba impersonalia*) do not name or refer to a person; e.g., *mi vo fatasu tomo itçuvari vo ivanu mono gia* (39 (69v) 'even if one were to die, one should not tell a lie,' *mono mo tabezu saqe mo nomaide ichinichi fataraqu mono ca?* (69v) 'is it possible to work all day without eating anything or drinking any wine?', *xujin no maie de sono ióna coto vo iú mono ca?* 'is it possible to speak this way in front of ones lord?' Concerning the conjugations for these verbs they follow the rules according to their roots.

The root of any verb of whatever conjugation can be taken from its conjugation and changed to another conjugation by adding one of the particles of honor (*honor*). The resulting form will belong to the conjugation determined by the final letter of the particle. These particles are: *maraxi,uru*, *ari,u*, *saxerare,uru*, *xerare,uru*, *nasare,uru*, *saxemaxi,u*, *tamai,ó*, *rare* and *re*.[115]

The particle *maraxi* does not add honor to that which is talked about, but rather it is used to speak honorably to those in front of us. For example; *cui,u* means 'I eat,'[116] but a servant in front of his master will not say *nezumi ga cúta* 'the mice ate the cheese'; he will rather say *nezumi ga cui maraxita*. By itself *cui,u* is in the third conjugation because its root ends in *ui*, but if *maraxi* is added it becomes a verb in the first conjugation. When we refer to something about a people (*natio*) we do not show honor to that word but only pay attention to the person we are speaking to by adding *maraxi* or not. For example, if we are addressing an inferior we say *Nan ban jin va core vo cuvanu*; but if we are addressing a person of nobility we say *Nan ban jin va core vo cui maraxenu* 'Europeans do not eat this.' When *ari,u* is added to the root of any verb it attaches a middling (*mediocris*) degree of honor; e.g., *modori aró ca?* 'are you going to come back?' If you add *vo* in front of the verb it is honored moderately (*satis*); e.g., *vomodori aró ca?* 'Your Lordship is going to come back?' *Tono sama vo xini atta toqi* 'when the master died,' *Deus cono xecai vo gosacu atta* 'God created the world.'[117] We use these particles when we are speaking with honored persons whom we like and with whom we are on friendly terms.

The particle *nasare,uru* gives the highest (*supremus*), or moderately great (*satis magnus*) honor and is placed after the root of the verb; e.g., *Deus cono xecai vo gosacu nasareta* 'God created the world.'

The particles *rare* and *re* add a middling and not a great amount of honor to the verbs to which they are added. The particle *rare* is added mainly when we are talking about someone who is absent. It is formed by taking the *nu* from the negative present and replacing (40 it with this particle; e.g., *aguerare,uru* means 'I offer' when the person to whom the offering is made requires a middling degree of honor and respect (*reverentia*). This verb coincides letter for letter with the passive but is distinguished from it by the cases which it governs. The particle *re* is placed after verbs of the second and third conjugation only; e.g., *iomare,uru* 'to read' and *naravare,uru* 'to learn,' said of a person having a good reputation. We speak in this way when speaking of those who are equal to us and the servants of our lord, but not of other servants, or nobles.

The particles *saxemaxi* and *xemaxi* give the same degree of honor as *ari,u* and *rare* or *re*. These particles are added to the root of a first conjugation verb,[118] or to the negative present from which the *nu* has been removed; *aguesaxemasu* 'he offers.' *Maxi,u* [*Xemaxi,u*] is added to the negative present of the second and third conjugation verbs after taking away *nu*; e.g., *iomaxemasu* 'he reads,' and *naravaxemasu* 'he learns.'

The particles *saxerare,uru* and *xerare,uru* attribute great honor. The first is added to the negative present of verbs in the first conjugation[119] after the *nu* is removed, and the second is added to the [other] negatives in the same way; e.g., *aguesaxeraruru* 'I offer,' *iomaxeraruru* 'I read,' *naravaxeraruru* 'I learn.' Because these forms coincide letter for letter with the honorific causative, the particle *ari,u* may be placed after the verb and the particle *vo* may be placed before to avoid confusion; e.g., *yomaxe aru* [*vo iomaxe aru*] 'I read' and *naravaxe aru* [*vo naravaxe aru*] 'I learn.'

The passive verb, concerning which see below, also permits the particle *saxerare,uru*; e.g., *viamavaresaxeraruru* (99v) 'I am honored.'

The particle *tamai,ó* bestows the highest honor. We use it when speaking of God, saints, kings, or generals. It is added to the roots of verbs and conjugated in the third conjugation. It is placed after the root of the passive form when referring to God; e.g., *Deus filio, umare tamŏ toqi* 'when the son of God was born,' *Deus agamerare tamŏ* 'God is honored.'

The particle *tate matçuri,u* makes the meaning of the verb to which it is added humble. It is placed after the root of affirmative verbs; e.g., *Deus vo gotaixet ni zonji tate matçuru coto va ichi sugureta jen gia* 'to love God is the supreme virtue.' This particle permits some degree of honor if *re* is added to it after the final *e* [*i*] has been changed to *a*. Thus, when speaking of the saints in respect to God, one says, (41 *Sancto Domingo, Deus vo gotaixet ni zonji tatematçurareta* 'St. Dominic loved God.'

The particle *maraxi* [*mairaxi*][120] is able to elevate to honor the particle *rare*; e.g., *tono iori cono coto vo Padre ni vataximairaxerareta* 'the lord gave it to the priest.'

### *Certain Verbs Which of Themselves Indicate Honor*[121]

*Mesare,uru* indicates any act which can be done, or which is properly done by a noble person (*persona nobilis*). This includes such things as eating, drinking, sailing, riding a horse, etc. *Vôxerare,uru* means that a noble person speaks. *Vomaraxi,uru* and *vomaraxi ari,u* mean that a noble person gives. *Voxe,uru* [*Vôxe,uru*] and *vôxe ari,u* mean that a middling person (*persona mediocris*) says or declares.

Verbs preceded by *vôxe* or *mexi* are given the same degree of honor by either; e.g., *vôxe tçuqerare,uru* 'I declare,' *mexi tçucavare,uru* 'I serve,' which have the same meanings as *tçuqerare,uru* and *tçucavare,uru*. To call someone we use *coi* with an inferior, with someone not quite as inferior we use *iorai*, with someone a little better we use *vaxei*, while *vogiare* is the superior way to call. *Gozare*, which means that your Lordship should come, and *gozarŏ* in the future tense are even more honorable ways to indicate the imperative. *Voide nasarei, voide nasareô*, or *voide nasarei caxi* mean 'might your Lordship come,' or 'Oh! would that your Lordship come.' *Cudasare,uru* means that a noble person gives. *Tamavari,u* means that a noble person gives to an inferior. *Tamóri,u* means that a middling person gives. *Mizzu vo nomaxete tamŏre* 'Give me a drink of water.' *Cudasare,uru* and *tamóri,u* mean that a humble person eats honoring his food. *Coximexi,u* and *qicoximexi,u* mean that a noble person eats and hears. *Voboximexi,u* and *voboximesare,uru* mean that a noble person thinks. *Saxerare,uru* means that a noble person does. *Nasare,uru*, *asobaxi,u*, and *asobasare,iuru* [*asobasare,uru*] mean that a noble person does what is proper to him such as hunting, writing, reading, or reciting. *Ii,ú* is used when the person addressed is humbler than the person or thing spoken to; (42 and *mexi,u* [*móxi,u*] means the person or the thing spoken to is addressed with honor. Therefore I would be incorrect were I to say *mi ni móxe* 'tell me!' I should rather say *mi ni iie*. I should not say *tono ni iie* 'tell it to the lord,' but rather *tono ni móxe*. *Mairi,u* means to go to a place to which honor should be shown; e.g., *iglesia ie maire* 'go to church!' *Cure,uru* and *toraxe,uru* mean to give in a way that humbles the person to whom the thing is given. *Cui,ú* means 'to eat' without showing respect (*respectus*); *mexi,u* also means 'to eat' but it is cultivated (*urbanum*); e.g., in addressing those deserving respect I will not say *mexi vo cui maraxita* but rather *mexi vo tabe maraxita* 'I ate.' *Mairi,u* or *vomairari,u* [*vomairi ari,u*] means that a middling person eats, while *agaraxerare,uru* and *voagari ari,u* are nobler ways to say this. *Qiqi,u* means to hear and *uqetamavari,u* and *uqetamóri,u* mean to hear in a way which honors the person heard; e.g., *goiqen vo uqetamŏtta* 'I heard your advice.' *Móxi ague,uru* means to speak in a way which humbles oneself while bestowing honor on the person being addressed. *Móxi ire,uru* means to speak between equals (*equales*). *Chómon xi,uru* means to listen to the word of God. *Goranji,zuru* or *goranjerare,uru* is to look at a noble thing. *Xi,uru* means to do in common way, *itaxi,u* means to do in a cultivated way, and *tçucamatçuri,u* means to do in a humble way.

### *Cautionary Remarks on the Conjugations of the Verb*[122]

The particle *nama* placed before any verb in any tense means that the action has been done poorly or in an incomplete manner; e.g., *nama aró* 'I wash poorly,' *nama iaqu* 'I am incompletely broiled.'

If the particles *tçui, cai, uchi, faxe, voi, ai,* and *tori*[123] are placed in front of a verb they do not change the meaning, but they add emphasis; e.g., *uchi cobosu* has the same meaning as *cobosu* 'I pour,' *faxe noboru* is the same as *noboru* 'I ascend,' *voxi comi,u* is the same as *comi,u* 'I enclose,' *ai cavari,u* is the same as *cavari,u* 'I am changed,' *tçui mavari,u* is the same as *mavari,u* 'I go around,' and *tori firogue,uru* is the same as *firogue,uru* 'I spread out.'

The particle *qitte* is the gerund in *Do* for the verb *qiri,u* and when it is placed after the roots of certain verbs it gives them great emphasis; e.g., *tanomiqitte* 'imploring with great prayers,' *vomoiqitte* (43 'assuming a strong resolution.' The verbs *tanomiqiri,u* and *vomoiqiri,u* are also used.

The particle *ma,* when placed in front of certain verbs and nouns, gives them a stronger meaning; e.g., *mamucai* 'quite present,' *macuroi* 'completely black.'

The particle, or better root of the verb, *macari,u,* when placed before verbs of motion, makes the verbs modest and a bit more cultivated; e.g., *macari noboru* 'I ascend,' *macari cudari,u* 'I descend,' and *macari i,iru* 'I am present.'

The particle *va* placed after a sentence confirms what has been said before, as one might boast of making a prediction; e.g., *fune va cuchinotçu ie iru va* 'the ship calls at Kuchinotsu; and, if he says so or not, I say so,' *aru va* 'see if it is not as I have said.'

The particle *aidani* means 'between' in the sense of the time consumed in performing an action; e.g., *agura aidani* [*aguru aidani*] 'while offering,' *iôda aidani* 'while he read,' *naravózuru aidani* 'while he will learn.'

The particle *ga* means 'but;' *só iú ga; nanto aró ca?* 'they say so, but will it be so?' or 'it may be so, but I don't know for certain,' *furi va furu mai ga, fune no dasu coto naró ca xiranu* 'it's not raining any more, but I still don't know if it will be possible to launch the boat or not,' *sono qinpen ni va gozaru mai ga; doco cara toraxeraruru zo?* (20)[124] 'there are probably none in the neighborhood, or in the surroundings, so from where can they be gotten?'

The particle *gotoqu* is added to the present, preterit, and future tenses meaning 'in the same way'; e.g., *coxiraiuru gotoqu* 'in the same way as you furnish or carry out,' *qiita gotoqu* 'as I heard.' The form is sometimes *ga gotoqu*; e.g., *móxita ga gotoqu* 'as he said,' *caracavózu ga gotoqu* 'as in jest I will tease or laugh at.' This same meaning is obtained with *iŏni*; *Nifon no catagui vo xirareta iŏni, vôxeraruru* (122v) 'he speaks as one who knows the customs of Japan,'[125] *mósu ióni* 'as I say.' The particle *furi* is also used for the same purpose; e.g., *toza no chijocu vo nogareôzuru tameni catana vo saita furi vo mixerareta* (123) 'he showed himself wearing his sword in order to avoid the danger of infamy.' *minu furi vo saxerareta* (123) 'he made it known that he did not see.'

The particle *saie* is used [with the negative] to mean 'not at all'; e.g., *mma saie nacatta* (118)[126] 'there are not any horses at all,' *cotoba saie xiranu mono* (118) 'he does not know how to speak at all,' *ji saie mixiranu mono* 'he does not know any letters at all.' This same particle is used for emphasis; e.g., *qiden to saie mŏxeba* (119) 'it would (44 suffice if you were to say that you are,' *Padre no tçucavaruru to saie móxeba* 'if only he had said that this was useful to the priest,' or one might say 'it would suffice if, etc.'

The particle *qere* is a confirmative particle which comes at the end of a sentence with the meaning 'therefore'; e.g., *maitta qere* 'therefore he came,' *sate só aru qere* 'finally this is the situation.'[127]

The particle *coso* is of great importance among the Japanese for they use it first in an adversative sense (*in sensu adversativo*); *core coso ió gozare* [... *iô* ...] 'he is truly good.'[128] If the sentence in which this particle is found ends in a verb, that verb ends in *e*, as in the example above. If the verb is in the preterit it ends in *re*; e.g., *yô coso gazattare!* (117) 'you are welcome! (*bene veneris!*).' The exceptions to this rule are when the sentence does not end in a verb or an adjective; e.g., *core coso xixó yô* [... *io*] (116) 'he is a true teacher,' when after the particle *coso* there is in the sentence a gerund in *e*, a permissive in *tomo*, or a potential preterit in *tçuró* or *zzuró*;[129] e.g., *vare coso iro iro xinro tçucamatçutte cutatireba toxiiórini nari maraxita* [... *cutabireba toxiiorini* ...] (117) 'suffering many and various hardships, I became an old man,' *vare coso corosaruru tomo* 'if I be killed,' *fara coso tattçurŏ* (117) 'he was perchance quite angry,' *sato chicaqereba coso fi ga miiure* (116) 'the fire is already seen because the village is so near.' This [last] sentence ends in *e* because it does not contain an exception to the rule. *Vóxerareta coto domo vo go côquai de coso gozarózure* (97) 'without doubt you will do penance for what you have said,' *catajiqe nŏ coso gozare* (97) 'I congratulate you very much and thank you.' If someone says, 'Who did that?' the answer is *Patre coso* [*Padre coso*] 'the Priest did.' If someone asks, 'is there anyone who did that?' and if he does not hear, or does not understand the answer, and asks again, the person who answered will say *Juan coso* 'I have already said it was John.'

When someone is careless about what was said, or when he has not heard something and asks again, the answer is; e.g., *tovoru na to iieba* 'I have already told you not to pass through,' *iome to iieba* 'I have already told you to read,' *Padre coso to iieba* 'I have already told you that it is the Priest.'

Adding the particles *maieni* and *saqini* to the negative present tense makes the construction affirmative; e.g., *iglesia ie mairanu maieni* (141v) 'before he goes to church.' They are also added to the affirmative future tense; e.g., *mairŏzuru tote no saqini* 'a little before (45 I come.'

The particle *tocoro* signifies the time during which the action indicated by the verb is done. It is placed after the verb; *taburu tocoro ni* 'when I was eating,' *tabeta tocoro ni* 'after dinner,' *tabeôzuru tocoro ni* or *tabeôzuru ni* 'when I will be eating.' It also serves as a reduplicative particle which denotes a reduplication to the degree possible; e.g., *jesu christo humanidad no von tocoro va* (121v)[130] 'Jesus Christ in so far as he was a man,' *vonore ga foxxezaru tocoro vo fodocosu coto nacare* (121) 'as you do not want done to you, do not do to others,' *fudai no tocoro vo vo iurusu* [... *tocoro vo iurusu*] (120v) 'I gave him his freedom,' *fito no acu no tocoro ni va dôxin xenu* (121v) 'I do not consent to the sins of man,' *utagó tocoro mo nai* (120v) 'there remains no place to doubt, or for doubt,' *nocoru tocoro mo nai* 'it does not remain any more,' *tçuini, sono tocoro ie mairózu* (121v) 'finally he will arrive at this place,' *fumbet ni voiobanu tocoro gia* (121v) 'there are some things which are not understood, or to which one's comprehension does not extend,' *nani mo nai tocoro vo iô qicoximexe* (120v) 'will your Lordship kindly eat from this littleness which is nothing.' From these examples it is possible to see the force of this particle.

The particles *tocoro, made*, and *made de gozaru* are often added to an utterance (*cadentia*). They do not have any special meaning and are the same as *coto de gozaru*; e.g., *naranu made* or *naranu coto de gozaru* mean the same as *naranu* 'it is not possible.' *Guijet tçucamatçurŏ to zonzuru coto va cacugo itasanu coto gia* (10v) 'the breaking of this friendship does not come to mind.' Here the *itasanu coto gia* is the same as *itasanu* alone.

The particle *madeio* is used to confirm what has been said; e.g., *caita madeio* 'that which I wrote, I wrote.'

The particle *toqi* when added to the present tense, forms a preterit imperfect; e.g., *jennin tachi va saigo ni voiobi tamó toqi va buji ni gozatta* 'when saints arrive at the time of their death, they are peaceful and quiet.'

Changing the *ta* of the preterit to *tçu* and the *da* of the negative to *zzu*[131] the meaning becomes 'I do it this way and then that way'; e.g., *mono vo caitçu, iôzzu, nando xite curasu bacari gia* 'I spend my life reading, writing and doing other things,' *tattçu itçu vocu iori zaxiqi ie ide zaxiqi iori vocu ie iri xitten battŏ xeraruru* (11v) 'standing and sitting, entering and departing, he stands up and falls down.' The particle *ri* gives the same meaning after the preterit; e.g., *xeqen no mono va netari voqitari nŏdari curasu bacari gia* (11) 'men of the world spend their lives sleeping, arising, and drinking,' *mazzu* (46 *ite niva vo mo facaxetari, cusa vo mo ficaxetari iroiro no xigoto vo ategŏte cosó mairŏzure* [... *coso* ...] (10v) 'I shall go and sweep out the courtyard (*atrium*), pull up the weeds, and then having dispensed with these things I shall go,' *ima cono io fuqe iuqeba nome ia, utaie ia fito bito motçu, utǒtçu sacamori suru* (129) 'when it already is late at night, urging themselves on to drink and sing, the men enjoy themselves dancing and singing.'

The particle *ie,* which is the root of the verb *ie iuru* [*ie:uru*][132] 'I can,' signifies, when placed before negative verbs, that the action expressed by the verb cannot be done; e.g., *ie iomanu* 'I cannot read.' This particle is also placed after the infinitive; e.g., *iomanu coto vo ienu* 'I cannot read.' *Iomi va ieide,* or *iomi mo ieide* 'since I could not read, or not being able to read' is also said. The infinitive sometimes acts as a substitute verb (*suppositum verbum*); e.g., *xinuru coto va vosoroxij* 'it is terrible to die.'

The particle *tai* 'I want' is added to the roots of verbs and signifies the desire to do the thing indicated by the verb; e.g., *mizzu vo nomi tai*[133] 'I want to drink some water,' *mizzu vo nomi tó gozaru* or *mizzu vo nomi tó zonzuru,* but these last two forms are more noble. Here is an example of the noble form in the negative, *tǒ mo nai*; e.g., *mizzu vo nomi tǒ mo nai* 'I do not want to drink water,' and *mizzu vo nomi tǒ mo gozaranu. Mairu tó mo zonjenu* means 'I do not want to go.' When the particle *tai* is added to adjectives, or verbs indicating a sensory act (*actionem sensitiuam*) in the first person,[134] the *i* is changed to *c*; and the verb *ari,u* is added and conjugated in the tense required by the sentence; e.g., *cuitacatta* 'I wanted to eat.' If the verb is in the second or third person, the *i* is changed to *g* and again the verb *ari,u* is added, or an honorific particle depending upon what the person deserves, or without it as an absolute form. But if the person is inferior, the *i* is changed to *c* as said before.

The particle *de* sometimes gives a subjunctive sense when it is added to nouns; e.g., *varãbe de xinda* 'he died a child, or when he was a child,' *vare ga buchófó de tofó mo gozanai* (163v)[135] [... *buchôfó* ...] 'since I am clumsy and not careful, nothing will work out in a way that will be harmonious.'

The particle *ió* 'way' is added to the roots of verbs and also to the verbs themselves. When the root governs the genitive, the verb governs the same case; e.g., *cono qiǒ no iomi ió va* 'the way of (47 reading this book,' or *cono qió vo iomu iǒ va*. In the first sentence *qiǒ* is in the genitive with the particle *no*; in the second sentence it is in the accusative with *vo* because *yomu* governs this case. *Tei* signifies an extraordinary and marvelous way of doing something; e.g., *machicanuru tei vo goron jerarei* (122)[136] 'might your Lordship observe the way that they are expectant.' Also, *arisama* means 'way,' *me mo aterarenu arisama gia* 'it is a way, or a form (*figura*), which is unable to be seen.'

*Sama* indicates the time of the action of the verb to which it is added while governing the case required by the verb. It is added to the root of the verb; e.g., *saqe vo nomi sama ni* (105) 'when he actually drank the wine,' *iado ie caieri sama ni* (105) 'when he returned home,' *fune iori agari sama ni* (105) 'when he actually disembarked from the ship,' *fune ni nori sama ni* 'when he actually boarded the ship.'

When there are in a sentence two verbs whose actions form a single action, the first verb is put into the form of the gerund in *Do*; e.g., *mizzu vo motte coi* 'bring some water, or come bringing water,' *fune vo voite coi* 'bring the boat here, or come poling the boat,' *core vo totte iqe* 'take this, or carry this and go.'

The gerund in *Do* when added to verbs of asking, giving, or doing, means that one is asking to know or to acquire the thing which is indicated by the verb to which it is added; e.g., *nifon guchi vo voxiiete cure io* 'teach me Japanese,' *sŏ voxerarete cudasaruru na* [*sŏ vôxerarete* ...] 'your Lordship ought not say that,' *Deus no coto vo catatte tamŏre* 'do me the favor of relating to me those things which pertain to God.'

The particle *mo* placed after the gerund in *Do*, whether it ends in *te* or *de*, means 'although'; e.g., *sŏ mŏxite mo* 'although you say so,' *ica fodo susumete mo, corobu mai* 'no matter how much you try to persuade me, I will not deny the faith.' They also use *sŏ mŏxeba atte mo* 'even if you say that,' *dŏxitemo cŏxitemo* (134v) 'what ever you do.'

If the particle *coso* (see above) is added to the affirmative gerund in *Do*; and, if the sentence ends in this particle, the sentence becomes negative; e.g., *mite coso* 'I did not see anything,' *atte coso* 'there is no way.' But if the sentence does not end in *coso*, it becomes affirmative (48 and emphatic; e.g., *mite coso gozare* (116) 'I certainly saw.' The verb ends in *e* according to the rule explained above when the particle *coso* was being discussed.

When the negative gerund in *Do*, which ends in *e*, is followed by *va*, *naranu*, or *canavanu* it expresses necessity or the impossibility of the contrary; e.g., *mairaide canavanu* (106v)[137] 'it is necessary to go,' *ivaide va no coto naredomo, nanto xô ca?* 'and if the thing which is said to be necessary happens, what shall I do?' *xitagavaide naranu* 'it is necessary to obey.' The same meaning, but with less strength, is obtained with the future of the affirmative or negative infinitive and the permissive subjunctive in *domo*; e.g., *mairŏ coto de gozatta redomo* (18)[138] 'although I should have gone,' *mairu mai queredomo* [... *qeredomo*] (18)[139] 'although I should not be going,' *mairŏ coto de gozanacatta redomo* (18) 'although I did not have to go.' They also use the negative gerund in *Do* to obtain the meaning of 'if not'; e.g., *òracio vo mŏsaide cú na* 'do not eat unless you have said your prayers.'

The gerund in *e* indicates an action already done; e.g., *mexi cúte coi* 'come after eating!' *cono qió ga caite gozaru* 'this book was written,' *chichi ni fumi vo cacaide cuiaxiú gozaru* [... *cuiaxú* ...] 'I am ashamed that I did not send a letter to your father,' *cono qió ga caite gozaranu* 'this book was not written.'

The particle *nagara*, when added to the root of a verb, forms a gerund in *Do* if it is followed by a verb indicating a repugnant or contrary action; e.g., *toganin Deus iori bacutai no go von, o uqetatematçuri nagara; caietta somuqi tatematçuru* [... *go von vo uqe* ...][140] 'sinners receiving, or even if sinners receive, benefits from God, they will offend him rather than be grateful,' *Jesu Cristo Deus de gozari nagara, fito ni taixite cruz ni cacaraxerareta* 'while Jesus Christ was a God, he was crucified for man.' *Nagara* is also added to nouns; e.g., *quantai nagara* (136v) 'although there was some lack of education,' *sannin nagara* (137) 'three at the same time, or even if there are three' *aqiraca nagara* (136v) 'although he is famous.' In this instance *aqiraca na* loses its *na* as do all the other adjectives that end in *na*.

The particle *iasui* is added to the roots of active and passive verbs to form the supine in *Tu*; e.g., *iomi iasui* 'easy to read,' *corosare iasui* 'easy to be killed.' The same thing is achieved by the following way of speaking; *iúte va vosoroxij* 'it is terrible to say,' *mite va* (49 *fuxiguina* 'it is admirable to see,' *iú vo mo vosoroxij* 'it is terrible to say.'

## The Adverbs

### *First Section*[141]

Adverbs are formed from adjectives ending in *ai* by changing the *ai* to *ó*; e.g., *fucó* 'deeply,' for those ending in *oi* by changing the *oi* to *ô*; e.g., *caxico* [*caxicô*] 'wisely,' for those ending in *ei* by changing the *ei* to *eô*; e.g., *xigueo* [*xigueô*] 'densely,' for those ending in *ui* by changing the *ui* to *ú*; e.g., *aiŭ* 'in danger,' and for those ending in *ij* by changing the *ij* to *iú*; e.g., *cavaiú* 'unhappily.'

### *Adverbs of Place*[142]

The interrogative pronouns are eight in number; *izzucu*[*?*], *izzucata*[*?*], *donata*[*?*], *doco?*, *dochi?*, *dochira?*, *dono tocoro*[*?*], and *dono fŏ?*, and they signify 'which place?' To these adverbs are added the particles *va*, *no*, *ni*, *ie*, *vo*, *cara*, and *iori* according to the case required, such as 'from where,' 'whither,' 'through which place,' 'in what place,' etc. *Made* can also be added to them with the meaning of 'to the limit of which'; *doco made ie iqó ca*[*?*] 'up to where will you go?' The interrogative particle, *ca?* or *zo*[*?*], is added to these questions but it is better to use *zo* rather than *ca* in sentences with an interrogative particle; e.g., *izzuru ie maitta zo* 'where did you go,' *dono tocoro vo tovotta zo* 'at which place did you cross,' *doco iori itta zo* 'through where did he enter,' *dochi cara qita zo?* 'from where did he come?', *donata va Pedro no iado zo*[*?*] 'which is Peter's house?', *doco ni voru zo*[*?*] 'where, or in what place is he?' One may respond in many ways; *cono tocoro*, *coto moto*, [*coco moto*], *core*, *conata*, *cochi*, *cochira*, *coco*, *cocora*, *cono cata*, *cono fŏ*, which mean 'here (*hic*)'; *sono tocoro*, *soco moto*, *sore*, *sonata*, *sochi*, *sochira*, *soco*, *socora*, *sono cata*, *sono fŏ* (50 which mean 'there (*istic*)'; *ano tocoro*, *asoco moto*, *are*, *anata*, *achi*, *achira*, *asoco*, *asocora*, *ano cata*, *anofó*, which mean 'there (*illic*).' To these particles are added the case particles. The interrogative adverbs with the case particles and *mo* added mean 'everywhere,' 'through every place,' or 'to every place,' e.g., *dono tocoro ie mo tovorŏ* 'I shall go everywhere,' *doco ni mo* 'everywhere,' *doco cara mo* 'from everywhere.' However, if, instead of *mo*, *nari tomo* is added the meaning becomes 'any place,' in a distributive sense; e.g., *doco ie nari tomo mairŏ* 'I shall go to each place individually.' The same meaning is obtained by *doco zo* with the case particles placed between the *doco* and the *zo*; e.g., *doco ni zo aru fodo ni* 'if someone is any place.' *Coco caxico* means 'here and there.' *Doco mo caxico mo* means 'the whole place.' The case particles are placed before *mo*; e.g., *doco ni mo caxico ni mo* 'in the whole place,' but after the adverb; e.g., *coco caxico ni* 'here and there,' *coco caxico ie doco, caxico iori* [*coco caxico ie* 'to here and there,' *coco caxico iori* 'from here and there'], etc.[143]

The particle *uie* means 'above.' The genitive case is placed before it; e.g., *fandai no uie ni voqe* 'place it on the table,' *cono uie va gozaru mai* 'it will not be above this,' that is to say 'it will not be better than this,' *sono uie ni* 'about that,' *sono uie no sata vo catari are* 'tell me about that,' *core va izzure iori mo uie de gozaru* 'one will not discover anything better than his,' that is to say 'this is the best.' *Xita* means 'below.' It governs the genitive; e.g., *fandai no xita ni voqe* 'place it under the table,' *micotoba no xita iori* (141v) 'when the king finishes speaking,' *voxita vo cudasarei* (141v) 'would your Lordship be so kind as to give to me that which remains of your drink.'

The particle *soba* means 'side' and governs the genitive; e.g., *fito no soba vo fanaruru* 'he separates himself from the side of another.'

The particle *maie* means 'before' and governs the genitive; e.g., *fito no maie vo tovoru* 'I pass in front of someone else,' *cacugo no maie* (141v) 'according to ones disposition,' *funbet no maie* (141v) 'as I believe, or think, or according to the sense (*iuxta sensum*).'

The particle *mavari* means 'around' and governs the genitive; e.g., *iglesia no mavari ni tçuchi vo nague sutçuru na* 'do not put earth around the church.'

The particle *uchi* means 'within,' and the noun which precedes it must be in the genitive; e.g., *iglesia no uchi* 'in the church,' *ano fito va, fito no uchi de va nai* 'that man is not among men,' that is (51 to say 'he is not a man,' *futacuchi cúta coto va, cúta uchi de va nai* (142v)[144] 'to eat two mouthfuls is not to eat.'

The particle *foca* means 'outside,' and the genitive is placed before it; e.g., *igelsia no foca ni* 'outside the church,' *foca ie iqe* 'go out, or go outside.' Sometimes the genitive particle is replaced by *iori*; e.g., *Deus vonago ichinin iori foca tçucuri tamavanu* (142v)[145] 'God did not create but one woman,' that is to say 'he created just one,' *Tengu fito ni acu vo susumuru iori foca va, nai* (142v) 'the Devil does nothing if he is not persuaded by man to sin,' *goxŏ vo tasucaru tame baptismo vo sazzucaru iori foca bechi no michi ga nai* 'there is no other way to save men than by baptism,' that is to say 'without baptism we cannot be saved.' *Deus no gracia iori foca* 'without the grace of God.'

The particle *naca* means 'in the middle.' It is used when the material is either dense or defuse; e.g., *qi no naca ni* 'in the wood,' *fito no naca ni* 'among the men.'

The particle *nacaba* means 'in the midst of things' when referring to a sequence. It follows the genitive; e.g., *dangui no nacaba ni* 'in the midst of the sermon,' *sore vo qijte, nacaba va vosore; nacaba va aqirete ita* (145v) 'hearing that, he feared and was afraid,' that is to say 'he spent most of his time being afraid.'

The particle *ato* means 'behind' and governs the genitive; e.g., *sonata no ato cara mairŏ* 'I shall come after you' that is to say 'I shall follow you.'

The particle *vaqi* means 'near' and governs the genitive; e.g., *Pedro no vaqi* 'near Peter,' *misa no vaqi* 'the mass is ended,' *cono vaqi* 'in the last few days.' All of these adverbs require after them the cases that are required by the verb which follows.

### *Adverbs of Interrogation and Response*[146]

There are many ways to ask 'why?' or 'for what reason[?]'; e.g., *najeni*[?], *najoni*[?], *nani xini?, nani tote ca?, nani no iuie ni?, nanto xita coto ni?, nani no xisai ni iotte?*. The question 'how?' is said; *nanto xite?, nanto iŏ ni*[?], *icani to xite?* The answer is 'because' or 'for the reason that'; e.g., *sono iuie va, najeni to iúni*. 'Because' is also said; *tocoro de, fodo ni, ni iotte*, or *sacai ni*. The first expresses (52 the greatest degree of causality, the second not so much, and the third the least.

*Uie va* means 'since (*cum* or *si quidem*)'; e.g., *toganai uie va qizzucai ga nai* (40v)[147] 'I am not afraid because I have no fault.' The same meaning is achieved by the particle *cara*; e.g., *caiŏ ni iro vo misuru cara va; cacusu coto va iranu* 'since you have thus shown your feelings (*iro*), you can't hide them.' 'Since (*si quidem*)' means approximately the same as *toqi va* and *xicaru toqi va*. *Sari nagara* means 'but,' *sari tote va* means 'until,' *saru tote va* means 'since the thing is this way,' *saru tote va, qicoienu coto gia* 'since it is so, it is unbearable.'

## *Adverbs of Time*[148]

One asks 'when' with *itçu* or *itçugoro*. One asks 'from what day' with *icca saqi* or *icca maie*, 'from what month' with *icutçuqi saqi*, and 'from what year' with *nannen maie*. Usually *ni* is added when it is required by the verb, and the interrogatives *ca* or *zo* are always put at the end of the sentence, with *zo* preferred.

One answers 'now' with *ima* or *tada ima*, and 'already' with *mŏ*, e.g., *mŏ iqe* 'be already gone!' 'Sometimes' is said with *toqi ni iotte* or *jibun ni iotte*. 'Afterwards' is *nochi*. *Sore cara* or *sore iori* means 'after that,' *core cara* or *core iori* means 'after this,' and *are iori* or *are cara* means 'after that.' 'Immediately' is said with *iagate*. 'Afterwards' or 'again' is *ima iori nochi*, *ima iori xite va*, or *ima iori igo*. 'This morning' is said with *qesa*. *Connichi* or *qio* [*qiô*] is 'today,' and *asu* or *miônichi* [*miónichi*][149] is 'tomorrow.' 'Tomorrow morning' is *asa*, *axitatô*, or *asatocu*, and 'tomorrow night' is *mionia* [*miŏia*]. 'Before' is *ijen* or *saqi ni*. 'Yesterday' is *qinô* or *sacujit*. 'The day before yesterday' is *vototoi* or *futçuca saqi ni*. 'Several days in the past' is *cono giŭ*. *Cono fodo* and *xenjit* have the same meaning, as does *xendo*. *Condo* means 'several days in the future.' 'The day after tomorrow' is *asatte* or *miógonichi*. 'Three days hence' is *xiasatte* or *miómiógonichi*. *Qiônen* [*Qionen*] or *cozo* means 'last year.' 'This year' is *cotoxi*. 'Two years ago' is *vototoxi* or *votodoxi*. 'Three years ago' is *sanuruvotodoxi* [*sannuru votodoxi*].[150] 'Immediately' is *tachimaqi* [*tachimachi*] (53 or *socuij ni* [*socuji ni*]. *Sunavachi* is also 'immediately.' *Tanteqi* is 'in a moment.'

*Itçumade?* means 'until when?' *Itçumademo* means 'always.' *Itçu cara* means 'after what time.' *Itçu iori* means 'from what time.'

## *Adverbs of Negation*[151]

*Iia* or *iia* [*iia iia*][152] means 'not.' *Só devanai* means 'it is not so.' *Iccana* or *iccanagueni* means 'by no means,' *iume iume* means 'not even in a dream,' *sarani*, *ichiien*, *catçute*, or *catçute motte* means 'in no way,' and *io*, *iomo*, or *iomo iomo* means 'without thinking'; e.g., *catçute mairu mai* 'in no way shall I come,' *iomo só va gozaru mai* (117v) 'it will in no way come to mind why it will be so.' When affirmative verbs are added to these adverbs they become negative; e.g., *iomo iomo to mŏxitareba vo mairi atta* (117v) 'although you said you would not go, you went,' *io mairó* 'in no way shall I go.'

### *Adverbs of Affirmation*[153]

*Nacanaca* means 'it is so,' *vó* means 'so,' when one agrees. *Gueni* or *gueni gueni* means 'it is thus'; e.g., *gueni gueni só mo aró* 'without doubt the situation is thus.' *Chódo* means 'at all.' *Saiŏni, sono bun, sono gotoqu, sŏ de gozaru, sore sore, massŏ gia,* or *xicato* means 'it is so.' *Mottomo* means that something is reasonably said. *Guioi no gotoqu* means 'as your Lordship believes, or says.' *Mochiron* indicates that a thing does not come in to doubt or discussion. *Nacanaca naru coto de gozaranu* means 'truly it is not possible.' *Nacanaca no coto* indicates a thing with which it is possible to agree. *Macotoni* means 'truly,' as does *xinjit* or *xinjitni*. *Xeimon* means 'I affirm by oath.' *Isasaca* or *isasaca motte* means 'not even a little,' and *issai* or *ixxet* means 'in no way, or by no means,' and when these particles are added to the affirmative they mean 'truly.'

(54

### *Comparative Adverbs*[154]

*Iori, iori mo,* and *iori mo navo* mean 'more' in a comparison. The person compared is in the nominative case and the person to whom he is compared is in the ablative with one of the particles which we have listed above; e.g., *Pedro va juan iori mo gacuxó de gozaru* 'Peter is wiser than John,' *soco ie noboru iori va; mairanu ga maxi gia* 'it is better not to go than to climb up there.' *Gotoqu, mama,* and *iŏni* are adverbs of similitude (*adverbia similitudinis*) and require the genitive for the thing with which the comparison is made. If the particle is preceded by a verb, no genitive is required; e.g., *no iama ie nari tomo qitai mama ni qite, nurureba, nugui suteraruru* (124v) 'if they were to go to the mountains or the plains wearing such clothes as they want to wear, they will have to take them off when they become wet on account of the water.' *Vomô mama ni, vomô gotoqu,* and *vomô iŏni,* mean 'as I think,' *cono mi no mama ni* 'according to his desires, or his pleasure.' *Fodo* means 'to such a degree as (*tantum*),' or 'just as (*quasi*)'; e.g., *qifen ano fito fodo no gacuxó de gozaru*[155] 'you are as wise as he,' *fara ga cudaru fodo ioi* 'he will recover as soon as he has a bowel movement,' *michi vo aruqu fodo cutabiruru* (123v) 'as I walk so I get tired,' *acai fodo ioi* 'the redder the better,' *xinuru fodo no vazzurai de va nai* 'this disease is not strong enough to cause death,' *fune ni mesaruru fodo naraba vare mo norózu* (124) 'if Your Lordship would take up the task of boarding the ship, so shall I,' *tamexi mo nai fodo ni atta to mǒsu* (124v) 'they say it was as if it had never been,' *voquru fodo araba sore ie mairǒzu* (124) 'if I am able to arrive at the state where I can get up from bed, I shall come to you,' *chicara no fodo vo mite* 'seeing the degree of his strength,' *fodo nó tçuita* 'he arrived in an instant,' *core fodo* 'as this,' *sore fodo* 'as that,' *are fodo* 'as that,' *vovoi fodo* 'while more,' *sucunai fodo* 'while less.'

(55

### *Superlative Adverbs*[156]

*Uie* means 'the highest'; e.g., *christian no voxiie va izzure iori mo uie de gozaru* 'the doctrine and faith of Christianity are supreme, or above all,' *cono saqe no uie va nai* 'there is no better wine than that.' *Ichi* or *daiichi* means 'supreme, or unique'; e.g., *gacuxǒ no uchi ni Sancto Thomas daiichi de gozatta* 'among wise men Saint Thomas was the best,' *core va are iori uie* 'this is superior to that.' The particle *xita* has the opposite meaning of 'inferior, or the lowest'; e.g., *xiqitai va anima iori xita de gozaru* (141) 'the body is inferior to the soul.'

### *Adverbs of Intensity and Exaggeration*[157]

*Ichidan*, *chicagoro*, and *iccǒ* mean 'intensely (*valde*)'; e.g., *chicagoro no vo cocoro gaqe de gozaru* 'this is the greatest care and diligence,' *sore va icco varui coto gia* 'this is extremely bad.' *Bexxite* means 'chiefly,' *tori vaqe* means 'especially,' *coto no foca* means 'rarely, or extraordinarily,' *icanimo* means 'intensely,' and *amarini* means 'too much.' As has been said, adverbs are formed from adjectives according to the rules above, and these adverbs mean adverbially what the adjectives mean adjectivally; e.g., *fucai* means 'deep,' and *fucó* means 'deeply.' *Icani mo xizzucani* means 'extremely quietly,' *tani coto ni* means 'extraordinarily,' and *xitatacani* or *guiósanni* means 'in a way that is to be feared' that is to say 'too much.' See the dictionary.[158]

## *Accumulative Adverbs*[159]

*Voxinabete* means 'universally'; *sôbet* means 'generally,' as do *tçuneni* and *sojite* [*sôjite*]; *feijeini* means 'regularly'; and *voioso, tabun, vocata, ioppodoni* mean 'for the most part,' and *qeccu* or *caiette* (56 means 'after all.' *Tennen* means 'perhaps,' as do *xijen* and *icasama. Sadamete* means 'probably,' *canarazu* means 'without doubt,' *moxi xijien* [*moxi xijen*] means 'perhaps,' *xŏtocu* means 'naturally,' *jinen* means 'by chance,' *xidai vidai ni* or *jen jen ni* means 'gradually,' and *vonozzucara* means 'by oneself.'

## *Adverbs that Conclude and Claim Attention*[160]

*Ficqiŏ* and *tçuini* mean 'finally, or in conclusion.' *Tçugŏ* means 'in summary.' *Nŏ nŏ* means 'is it not so?' e.g., *nŏ nŏ icani qicaxeruru ca?* 'do you hear me then?' *Moxi*[161] means 'ho there (*heus*),' but it is an elegant word; e.g., *moxi Padre sama* 'ho there, Reverend Father.' *Iare* also means 'ho there,' but with inferiors; e.g., *iare tarŏ quaja to iieba* 'saying "Ho there, Tarōkaja."' *Iai* means 'ho there' with very low people; e.g., *iai sochi ga motta mono va nani zo?* 'hey! what is it that you bring?' *Ia* has the same meaning; e.g., *ia vo tono bara domo va nani vo savagu zo?* (128) 'hey! you soldiers and good men, why do you quarrel?' The particle *ai* has the same meaning but it is placed after the sentence; e.g., *izzure mo mina qiqe ai* (129) 'hey! all of you listen.'

The particles *ca* and *zo*, as has been said above, are used as interrogatives. The particles *ia* and *caia* have the same function but they are more humble; e.g., *are va tare caia?* 'who is he?', *core ia*[*?*] 'this?', *io fuqete tare ca va tazzuneô zo?* (89v) 'when it becomes late at night, who will be able to visit?', *sore de arŏ ca to iú coto gia* 'I said, "will it be this?"'

*No?* asks for agreement; e.g., *gozarŏ ca no?* 'will he come?'[162] *mairŏ to voxerareta no?* [... *vôxerareta no?*] 'did he say that he will come?' *no Pedro dono?* 'isn't that so, Peter?' *Na*[*?*] means the same thing, but it is used with inferiors; e.g., *sŏ qiita na?* 'didn't you hear so?' Sometimes, in a sentence containing *zo, baxi*, which is a dubitive particle (*particula dubitandi*), is placed; e.g., *nanto xita xisai de baxi gozaru zo?* (122v)[163] 'for what reason did this happen?', *sate nanto iú voqiacu de baxi gozaru zo*[*?*] (123) 'what is the name of your guest?', *goiô baxi gozaru ca?* 'isn't there something of use to you?'

*Io* and *zo* strengthen or give cadence to the sentence; e.g., *caita zo* 'he truly wrote,' *maitta io* 'he certainly came,' *sono toqi vare* (57 *va ichi dan varui tçucai vo xiraruite gozaru io* [... *siaruite* ...] (95) 'at that time I was following bad advice.' *Bacari* means 'only, or in only one way,' *sore ni caguitte* means 'that only,' *core ni caguirazu* 'not only this.' *Bacari* also means 'more or less'; e.g., *fiacu bacari* 'there were a hundred,' *fiacunin bacari corosareta* 'about one hundred men were killed.' *Nó, nóte, naqu xite,* and *naqute* mean 'without'; e.g., *raxxi mo nó* 'without reason or order,' *cacugo nó* 'without any preparation.'

The adverbs of sound (*adverbia sonus*) are many and vary in accordance with the way that the Japanese perceive the sound. The particle *to* is added to them; e.g., *va va to xite* 'vociferously saying *wa wa,*' and if they add *meqi,u,* it means to make even a louder noise; e.g., *va meqi,u* 'to shout saying *wa*.'

### *The Case Prepositions*[164]

*Tame* or *ni* means 'concerning';[165] e.g., *sonata no tame* 'for you (*tibi*).' It governs the genitive which precedes it; *nan no tame* 'for what,' *nani ni naru ca?* 'for what is it?', *nani ni xô ca?* 'what do you do that for?', *nani no iô ni tatçu ca?* (171v) 'for what is it needed, or useful?', *maitte no iô va?* (130) 'what's the use of going?'

*Tai xite* means 'on account of' or 'against'; e.g., *tengu ni tai xite teqito* 'to fight against the devil, or resist him,' *Deus ni tai xite cuguio vo coraiuru* 'I endure the pain (*labor*) because of God.' *Uie iori* also means 'because'; e.g., *von jifi no uie iori* (167) 'because of his mercy.'

*Ni iotte* signifies the reason for which; e.g., *Deus iori fito no jento acu ni iotte go fempô vo ataiesaxerareozu* [... *ataiesaxerareôzu*] (146v) 'God gives to man according to his virtues and vices.' This form is derived from the verb *iori,u.*

*Ni tçuite* means 'around, or about' and is derived from the verb *tçuqi,u*; e.g., *core ni tçuite, core ni tçuqi,* or *core ni tçuqete* means 'about that.' *Sono gui ni voite va zonjenu* (120) 'I do not know anything about this matter,' *Vôxe va mottomo naredomo vagami ni totte va canai gatai* (120) 'Your Lordship speaks well but what concerns me is that (58 it is difficult to do.' *Dai quan ni itatte va ichinin bacari sadame io* (120)[166] 'decide that which concerns the steward only.' *Itatte* and *totte*[167] are the gerunds of verbs just as the preceding. They also say *Padre coto va* 'the things belonging to the priest,' *varera coto va* 'about my things, or those things which belong to me.' *Xitagatte* or *xitagŏte* means 'near' and is the gerund of the verb *xitagari,u* or *xitagai,ó*. As with the other verbs it governs the dative case; e.g., *guioi ni xitagatte* or *xitagŏte* 'according to Your Lordship's understanding.' *Xidai* has the same meaning; e.g., *conata xidai* 'according to your wishes.' Sometimes it is added to the roots of verbs; e.g., *mairi xidai* 'according to when he comes, or according to his coming.'

*Ni* indicates the place in which. *Ni voite* has the same meaning but indicates permanence; e.g., *fatto va fuximi ni voite vôxeidasareta* 'he established the law while he was in Fushimi,' *Bungo funai ni itatte* 'in the city of Funai in the kingdom of Bungo,' *iglesia ni uoru* 'he is in church.'

*De* indicates the place of an action; e.g., *michi de Pedro ni vŏta* 'I met Peter in the street.' The same particle *de*, together with *vo motte*, indicate the instrument with which an action is done; e.g., *bo vo motte Pedro vo uchi coroita* 'he killed Peter with a stick,' *Padre sama catarareta de navo qicoieta* 'from what the Reverend Father told me, it became easier to understand,' *necqi de xinda* 'he died of a fever.'

*Cara* or *iori* indicate the place from which; e.g., *iglesia cara* 'from church.' They also say *fune cara maitta* 'he came by ship' and *cachi cara maitta* 'he came on foot.' *Fune de maitta* is the same as *fune cara maitta* and *fune ni notte maitta*. *Fana cara me cara miguruxij mono gia* 'it is unpleasant to the nose and the eyes.' *Iori* indicates the place through which; e.g., *sama iori faitta* 'he entered through the window.'

*Tomo ni* means 'at the same time'; e.g., *sonata to tomo ni mairŏzu* I shall go at the same time as you,' *mŏsu to tomo ni* 'at the same time as he spoke.'

*Ie* indicates the place to which; e.g., *achi ie mairŏ* 'I shall go directly to court (*curia*),' *miiaco no cata ie noboru* 'he went up to court' and also *miiaco no fŏ ie noboru*. They also say *miiaco no iori, miiaco sama*, or *miiaco no gotoqu noboru*, but this is not a good way of speaking and is more characteristic of a rustic (*rusticus*).

*De* indicates the material from which; e.g., *tçuchi de cavara* (59 *vo tçuquru* 'to make bricks out of earth or mud,' *nande core vo tçuquru ca?* 'from what is this made?'

*Uie* means 'concerning'; e.g., *zuibun codomo no uie vo fito ni mo naxi marasuru iŏni to cocoro gaqe marasuru* 'with great diligence I took care of my sons so as to make them men.' *Sonata no fiquan no vo saiban mesare io* [... *no uie vo* ...] (141) 'take care of your servants.'

*Made* means 'until'; *asu made* 'until morning,' *inochi vo uxinŏ made aru mai* 'he will not lose his life, or he will not arrive at the loss of his life,' *sore made vomoi mo ioranu gui gia* 'it will not come to my mind,' *cocoro zaxi areba canavanu made mo xei vo iruru* 'when something is wished for, one uses his strength up to the point of impossibility,' *mŏsu made mo nai* 'it is not necessary to say,' *cono tocoro made maitta* 'I came to this place.'

*Conjunction and Separation*[168]

*To* means 'and'; e.g., *Pedro to juan to Nagasaqi ie ita* 'Peter and John went to Nagasaki,' *core to, are to vo toru* 'I take this and that.' *Mo* has the same meaning; e.g., *Pedro mo juan mo Nagasaqi cara modotta* 'Peter and John returned from Nagasaki,' *naqu mono mo ari, varó mono mo aru* 'there are those who cry and those who laugh. *Mo* is often placed before negative verbs; e.g., *nanigoto mo gazaranu ca?* 'is that not something new?'

*Mata* means 'and,' whether it is found between nouns or verbs. *Ca* means 'or'; e.g., *Pedro ca; juan ca coi to iie* 'tell Peter or John to come.' *Arui va* also means 'or'; e.g., *arui va Pedro, arui va juan* 'either Peter or John,' *arui va iomu, arui va caqu* 'I either read or write.' *Moxi va* means 'if in fact,' and it is used in the middle of a sentence; e.g., *moxi va cane ga nai naraba* 'if in fact you were to have no money.'

*Mata va* is used to bind the sentences more tightly together (*ad orationem contexturam*). It means 'besides that, or besides'; e.g., (60 *arui va iamai ga vocoru ca, mata va isogui no fumi qitaru ca etc.* [... *ca*, etc.] (135) 'either some sickness occurs, or besides that some urgent letter arrives.'

*Xicareba* means 'since things are this way,' *sari nagara* means 'but,' *sŏ aru tocoro de* means 'since it is thus,' *saraba* means 'since it is so,' and *sareba sareba* means 'since then.' *Ca?* means 'if'; e.g., *maitta ca mi io* 'see if he came, or went,' *maitta ca xiranu* 'I don't know if he went.' *Iara* means 'if,' but distributively (*divisive*); e.g., *fito iara chicuxŏ iara xiranu* 'I don't know if it's man or beast,' *nani iara to mŏxita* 'I wonder what he said.'

Some disjunctive and emphatic particles are formed from *nanica* and *tocacu* with the addition of other particles; e.g., *nani ia ca ia?* 'which thing?' The same meaning is expressed by *nani iara ca iara?* and *nanto iara cato iara? Nanto xite, cato xite* means 'how,' *nanto mo cato mo* means 'in no way,' and *nani mo ca mo* means 'nothing.' *Nanigoto mo cagoto mo, mina içtuvari naru zo* [... *itçuvari* ...] 'when all is said and done they are all lies.' *Nani no ca no*, and *nanto xite, cato xite* are ways to excuse oneself. *Nani no ca no to iúte* means 'saying this and that.' *Domo como* means 'in whatever way it is,' as does *dŏ xite mo cŏ xite mo*. *Dŏ xite cŏ xite* means 'doing this and that differently.' *Dŏ xô cŏ xô* means 'I shall do this and that.'

*Tomo cacumo* means 'all the same,' as do *toni cacuni, tonimo cacunimo*, and *totemo cacutemo. Core to ij; care to ij* means 'saying this and that, or making excuses.' *Care core* means 'this and that,' *coco caxico* means 'here and there (*hic and illic*).' *Vomoxirô, vocaxu*[169] [*vomoxirovocaxŭ*] is used when accommodating oneself almost to flattery.

If the particle *motte* is added to the particles *catçute, isasaca, tomoni, nani*, and *nani nani iori* [... and *nani iori*] it adds strength and force; e.g., *catçute motte sŏ aru mai* 'the situation will not be this way at all.'

### *Interjections*[170]

*Sate, sate sate,* [*satemo,*] and *satemo satemo* are interjections of admiration; e.g., *satemo Deus no voqinaru vonjifi cana* 'oh! great mercy of God!'

*Avare* is the interjection for pity; e.g., *avare mutçucaxij io no naca cana* 'oh! world replete with misery!'

*Ha!*[171] is the interjection of penetence; e.g., *ha faxi demo* (61 *vomoxiroi ga; tocoro ni iote qicoie canuru* [... *ni iotte* ...] (127v) 'ah, the workmanship of the sound and the harmony of the singing is most graceful, but it is not able to be heard well.'

*Iara!* is the interjection for joy and pain; e.g., *iara iara medeta ia* (128) 'oh! how much I rejoice.' *Ia* is also used; e.g., *satemo iiaxii iatçubara ia* (129) [172] 'oh! how vile and despicable,' *gongo dŏdan fuxigui na xisai cana* (128v) 'oh! how rare and ridiculous a reason.' *Iei* is the interjection of wonder; e.g., *iei Padre sama cochi gozaru io* 'oh! here is the Reverend Father.'

*Hat* is the interjection that indicates that one is repentent; e.g., *Benqei core vo mite hat coto naxi to zonjite, sono mama niva ni bŏ vo voraxi,* etc. (127v) 'Benkei seeing this,' etc.[173]

### *The Syntax and the Cases that are Governed by the Verbs*[174]

The nominative is placed at the beginning of the sentence and the verb at the end: the remaining elements are placed according to the cadence (*cadentia*) of the sentence; e.g., *Pedro va Nagasaqi de xutrai xita iqi iqi ni tçuite juan vo coroita* 'Peter killed John because of an argument that took place in Nagasaki.' In certain sentences of serious import a substitute verb (*verbum suppositum*) is placed after the verb, but this is rare; e.g., *tare mo canavanu futari no qimi ni tçucŏru coto va* (84)[175] 'no one can serve two masters.' In this sentence the substitute verb is *tçucŏru coto va*. *Core ni iote tanomi tatematçuru itçumo virgen* [*Core ni iotte ...*] (84) 'therefore I pray to the ever virgin [Mary].'

Clauses (*orationes*) in the absolute or permissive subjunctive, infinitive, conditional, and causative are always placed before clauses that are in the indicative or imperative, even if it does not make sense in Latin or any other European language; e.g., *achi cara tomeraruru tomo; tomaru na* 'do not stay, even if they want you to remain,' *sore vo qiitareba, fara vo tatete modotta* 'when he heard that, he came back very angry,' *taxicani uqetamotta ni iotte coso, móxi ague maraxitare* 'I listened carefully, and then I spoke,' *faiŏ gozatta raba vo mexi vo xinjô mono vo* 'if you had come earlier, I would have offered you food.'

When there are two verbs in the same sentence, the first will (62 be in the gerund form and the other will be in the tense that is required by the sense of the sentence; e.g., *core vo totte giqi ni mi ga comono ni vataxe* 'take this and give it to my servant at once.'

When there are two or more clauses which have the same subject or tense, only the last verb will be in the tense that is required by the sense of the sentence. The other verbs will be in the root form, while still others will be in the gerund in *e* form; e.g., *tovazunba cotaiezu, voxe raba tçuxxinde qiqi* [*tovazũba ... vôxe ... qiqe*] (85v)[176] 'if they don't ask don't answer: if they speak listen carefully,' *Deus no vo coto vo macoto ni uqe, go voqite mo camavaide, sono mama inferno ni vochita* 'he did not believe in God, and he did not respect His precepts; therefore, he fell into Hell.'

Verbs are always placed in the third person to indicate honor. No one honors himself except the king when he is speaking of himself; e.g., *iorocobi ni voboximesu* 'I am enjoying it very much.'

When there are many adjectives in a sentence, they will all be in the adverbial form except the last; e.g., *qe nangŏ, iro curô, icanimo utçucuxij mono* [*qe nagŏ ...*][177] 'a very beautiful person with long, black hair.'

The particle *to* is placed before verbs of understanding, believing, and hearing, takes the place of the verb 'to be,' and means 'that'; *fito to zonjita* 'I thought, or believed that he was a man,' *qixó vo jennin to vomovô ca?* [*qixo ... vomovŏ ca?*] 'shall I believe that you are a saint?' *Amata no fito xini no fonovo ni moiuru vo misaxerareô* (20)[178] 'you will see many men burning in the flames of indignation.' Here one has replaced *to* with *moiuru vo*, which is a substitute verb. When *mo* is added to *to* it strongly affirms what is said; e.g., *mairó to mo* 'I shall certainly go, or I will be going.'

The particle *to*, in the first meaning, is sometimes replaced by *iŏni*; e.g., *agueta iŏni gozaru* 'they say that he offered it,' *ica iŏna fito to va xiranu* 'I did not know what kind of a man he was.' Sometimes the substantive verb takes the place of the particle *to*; e.g., *mairó de gozatta* 'he said that he would come,' *xô de va naqeredomo* 'although I did not say that I would do it.'

*Qiuzo core vo mite, ima vo saigo no coto de areba* (97)[179] 'seeing this, Kiso believed that the hour of death was present, etc.' Here the substantive verb replaces *to* and serves as an active verb governing the accusative *ima vo*, which also replaces *to*. The particles *sŏna* and *guena* mean 'it seems.' *Sŏna* is added to the roots of verbs; e.g., *deqi* (63 *sŏna* 'it seems that it is finished.' If a substantive verb is placed after this particle the *a* is changed to *i*; e.g., *deqi sŏni gozaru* 'it seems that he will finish,' *deqi sŏni mo zonjenu* 'I believe that it will not be finished.'[180] *Sŏna* is also added to adjectives in *i*, and when it is the *i* is lost; e.g., *io sŏna* 'it seems good, or it seems that it is good,' *xigue sŏna* 'it seems dense,' and *aiau sŏna* 'it seems that I am in danger.' If this particle is added to adjectives in *na*, the *na* is lost; e.g., *aqiraca sŏna* 'it seems that it is clear.'

The particle *guena* is added to the nouns and verbs previously formed; e.g., *maitta guena* 'I believe that he has come.' If a substantive verb is added to this particle the *a* changes to *i*; e.g., *maitta gueni gozaru* 'I believe that he has come.' *Sŏna* means 'it seems,' and *guena* means 'I believe,' but either of these forms may occasionally be used in any of the examples given.

When a sentence has two preterits, the first may be in the preterit and the second in the future; e.g., *qesa cara sŏ vôxerareta raba mo faia de maraxô* 'If you would have said that this morning, I would have already left.'

When reporting what someone else has said, it is said this way; *Padre mósaruru va: iagate sonata ie mairó to mŏsaruru* 'the priest said that he was going to come.' Sometimes when one is excusing himself he will use *no* in place of *to*; e.g., *asu no, raiguat no, nando to noburu na* 'don't spread around that it is tomorrow, next month, or whenever.'

When *vo* follows *n* it loses its *v*; e.g., *go von o uqetatematçutta* 'I received benefits.'[181]

Adverbs are always placed before their verbs except for the adverbs of time which are placed at the beginning of the sentence; e.g., *sore vo qijte iccó xicari maraxita* 'hearing that he was very angry,' *qiô nen espana cara vatatta toqi* [*qio nen* ...] 'when I sailed from Spain last year.' Each verb requires before it a subject in the nominative case, either expressed or understood; e.g., *vare iqe* or *iqe* 'come!', where the *vare* is understood. In some sentences this rule is not respected; e.g., *xisai voba core ni mósare maraxozu* [... *maraxôzu*] 'he will explain, or give the reason for this.' In the following case we do not see the nominative, but rather *are ni va*, which is in the dative or ablative; *are ni va, navo voixri atta* [... *voxiri atta*] 'he knows better.' In this sentence the *are ni va* ought to be in the nominative. *Cacaru vo ni va cogane no cusari vo icusugi mo tçuqeta dógu de gozaru* (138v) 'for a necklace (*torques*) he had a chain of gold with many links.'

*Core ni va gozonji aru mai* 'Your Lordship does not know (64 about this.' Here the *core ni va* replaces the accusative which is governed by *zonji,uru*.

The impersonal verb or the infinitive requires a nominative before it; e.g., *Pedro va maitta to mósu* 'they say that Peter came.'

The verb *iri,u*, which means 'to need,' governs two nominatives, one for the thing and the other for the person in need; e.g., *vatacuxi va cono cane ga iru* 'I need, or I have a necessity for this money.' It also governs the dative for the person; e.g., *sono tame ni va cane ga iranu* 'he does not need any gold, or money.'

The active verb requires the accusative before it; e.g., *cane vo motanu* 'I have no money.'

Certain *cobita* or *coie* nouns, as we have said above, are borrowed from Chinese and govern the same cases as the Japanese verbs to which they correspond; e.g., *niva vo qenbut no aida ni mexi vo coxiraie io* 'prepare the food while we visit the garden.' The noun *qenbut* requires the accusative *niva vo*. The same is true with *fito ni guenzan suru* (97) which is like *fito ni vó* 'I meet the man.' The *guenzan* governs the dative just as does the verb *ai,ó*.

When a borrowed word (*vocabulum cobitum*)[182] is a compound of two elements it is possible to determine if it is a verb by seeing if the first part has the meaning of a verb; e.g., *jóten* is a verb which means 'to ascend to heaven' with the *jŏ* meaning to 'go up.' *Tenjŏ* is a noun in which the *jŏ* is placed after the *ten* and means 'heaven.'

The passive verb has the ablative for its agent (*persona agente*); e.g., *Pedro cara corosareta* 'he was killed by Peter,' but it is better that it govern the dative; e.g., *Pedro ni corosareta*, or *Pedro va nusubito ni cane vo torareta* 'Peter had his money stolen by thieves.'

There are also certain neutral verbs which govern the accusative as if they were active verbs; e.g., *xiqitai vo fanaruru* 'to depart from the body, or to die,' *axi vo vazzuró* 'to have a pain in the foot.' This is also true for *nigue,uru* 'to escape,' *nogare,uru* 'to evade,' *de,uru* 'to go out,' *noqe,uru* 'to retreat,' *tovori,u* 'to go across,' *nori,u* 'to sail,' as in *caixŏ vo noru* 'I sail the sea,' *iuqi,u* 'to walk,' as in *michi vo iuqu* 'I walk the streets,' *vovari,u* 'to finish,' *mairi,u* as in *xogui vo mairu* 'I play chess (*tabula laterucularia*),' *iorocobi,u* as in *cocoro vo iorocobu* 'I gladden the heart,' *abi,uru,* as in *mizzu vo abiru*[183] 'I wash myself with water, or I pour water on myself,' *avaremi,u* 'I am sad,' (65 *canaximi,u* 'I am unhappy,' *coie,uru* 'to cross over,' *fabacari,u* 'to be shy,' *facarai,ŏ* 'to take care of,' *faxiri,u* 'to sail,' as in *caixŏ, vo, faxiru* [*caixŏ vo faxiru*] 'I sail the sea,' *fagi,zzuru* 'to be ashamed,' *fedate,tçuru* 'to separate,' *fe,uru* 'to spend,' as in *ficazu vo furu* 'I spend many days,' [*fumaie,uru* 'to be based on,' as in] *dori vo fumaiuru* 'to be based on reason, or to have reason as a basis,' *itami,u* 'to be sick,' *mavari,u* 'to go around,' as in *cono cotovari vo móxi mavatta* 'he goes around and spreads the news here and there,' *meguri,u* has the same meaning, *nagusami,u* 'to please,' as in *cocoro vo nagusamu* 'I make the heart happy,' *naqi,u* 'to weep,' *tasucari,u* 'to be saved,' as in *inochi vo tasucaru* 'I am saved from the dangers of life,' or *goxŏ vo tasucaru* 'to be saved for a future life,' *tachi,tçu* 'to go away from,' as in *tocoro vo tatçu* 'I go away from this place,' *tomurai,ó* 'to make a funeral for the dead,' *ucagai,ó* 'to inquire with hesitation,' *voximi,u* 'to value,' *urami,u* 'to enquire,' *xinobi,u* 'to wait in hiding, almost insidiously,' as in *fito no me vo xinobu* 'I am careful lest someone see me.'[184] A few of these verbs which require the accusative of location admit to the use of the ablative with the particles *cara* or *iori*; e.g., *tocoro vo tatçu* is the same as *tocoro iori tatçu* 'I leave the place.'

There are some active verbs which require two accusative cases; e.g., *fori,u, daxi,u, fanaxi,u, tate,tçuru*. For example, *Pedro vo soco vo voi idaita* 'they led Peter away from that place.' It is possible that it governs the ablative of location; e.g., *Pedro vo soco cara voi daita* [... *voi idaita*]. Some take either the dative or the accusative; e.g., *fito vo,* or *fito ni fanare,uru* 'to go away from the men,' *Deus vo,* or *Deus ni somuqi,u* 'to offend God.' Verbs of this kind are generally verbs of fearing, offending, or going away.[185]

Many verbs of helping, harming, damning, obeying, recognizing as superior or inferior, being subjugated, being victorious, and similar verbs govern the dative; e.g., *chiie saicacu iŏni coieta* 'he is superior to others in wisdom and industry.'[186]

Verbs of giving, promising, and the like, govern the accusative for the thing and the dative for the person; e.g., *fito ni cane vo cururu* 'to give money to someone.'[187]

There are many verbs which permit before themselves the roots of other verbs without change, letting the roots take on the function of an infinitive; e.g., *qiqi fajime,uru* 'to begin to hear.' Some of these verbs are: *nare,uru* 'to become accustomed,' *tçuqe,uru* with the same (66 meaning, *fate,tçuru* 'to finish,' *narai,ó* 'to learn,' *some,uru* 'to begin,' *todoqe,uru* 'to continue,' *ate,tçuru* 'to direct,' *atari,u* 'to find by chance,' *vaqe,uru* 'to divide,' *cane,uru* 'to be able to do with difficulty,' *soconai,ŏ* 'to be wrong,' *sumaxi,u* 'to finish,' *sugoxi,u* 'to exceed,' *fague maxi,u* 'to work much and intensely,' *aqi,u* 'to become bored,' *tai* 'to want,' and *tŏ mo nai* 'to not want.'[188] If the roots of verbs are placed before certain adjectives ending in *i*, they form a kind of supine in *Tu*; e.g., *iomi iasui* (92) 'easy to read (*facile lectu*),' etc.

A numeral, if a substantive noun is placed after it, must be in the genitive case; e.g., *fitotçu no toga* 'one sin.' The same is true with the particle *fodo* when it means 'all'; e.g., *aru fodo no fito* 'how so ever many.' The same is true with *iori*; e.g., *Nanban iori no mono* 'things from Europe.' But this is a relative formation (*relatiuum*). The genitive is also required with nouns that mean much or little; e.g., *amata no fito* 'many men.' These nouns are; *bechi* 'other,' *fon* 'one's own,' *cazucazu* 'many,' *sama zama* 'many ways.' *Iro iro* 'much' is the same as *iorozzu* and *izzure*. *Issai* means 'all,' as does *vono vono*, *cotogotoqu*, and *reqi reqi* for a noble person, *igue* 'that which follows,' *nocori* 'that which remains,' *itçumo* 'always,' *itçumo no coto* 'that which always is,' *tçune* 'usual,' *ima* 'now.' *Isasaca* means 'a little,' as does *soto* or *sucoxi*, *xotocu* 'natural,' *sono foca* 'others.'[189] These nouns are in the genitive if they are followed by a substantive noun, but when they are not followed by a noun they must be taken as adjectives. If they are followed by a verb rather than a noun, they do not require the genitive; e.g., *iorozzu dancŏ xite iocarŏ* 'it will be good if you all confer.'

# Japanese Arithmetic and Numerical Matters Concerning Which Much Painful Labor Is Required

There are two ways to count in Japanese.[190] The first is with the ordinary numerals which are called *iomi*. With these one is able to count to ten; e.g., *fitotçu* means 'one,' which is also used to (67 say 'a little,' as in *saqe fitotçu nomaxite tamŏre* 'give me a little sake to drink.' *Futatçu* means 'two,' *mitçu* 'three,' *iotçu* 'four,' *itçutçu* 'five,' *mutçu* 'six,' *nanatçu* 'seven,' *iatçu* 'eight,' *coconotçu* 'nine,' and *tovo* 'ten.' *Icutçu* means 'what?' and is used when one does not have the proper number.

The second way of counting is with the *coie* vocables which are borrowed from Chinese. These numbers are not used by themselves to count to ten; but are rather used when counting things which are represented by Chinese, and not Japanese vocables. These bound numerals (*termini numerales*) are: *ichi* 'one,' *ni* 'two,' *san* 'three,' *xi* 'four,' *go* 'five,' *rocu* 'six,' *xichi* 'seven,' *fachi* 'eight,' *cu* 'nine,' *jú* 'ten.' The numbers eleven and above are made by joining these numbers together. Thus, 'eleven' is *jŭichi*; *júni* is 'twelve,' *júsan* 'thirteen,' *júcu* 'ninteen.' The tens are obtained by placing one of the numbers in front of ten; e.g., *nijú* 'twenty,' *sanjú* 'thirty,' *sanjŭichi* 'thirty-one,' *cujŭ* 'ninety.' *Fiacu* means 'hundred,' *fiacu ichi* 'one hundred and one,' *fiacu jŭ* 'one hundred and ten,' *fiacu sanjŭ* 'one hundred and thirty,' *ni fiacu* 'two hundred,' *sambiacu* 'three hundred.' *Xen* means 'thousand,' and *xen roppiacu sanjŭ ichi* is 'sixteen thirty-one.'

By placing the Japanese numerals in front of Japanese vocables, which are called *iomi*, and by removing the *tçu* of the aforementioned numbers before they are joined to nouns or verb stems, one is able to enumerate those things which are indicated by the vocable; e.g., *fito cotoba* 'one word,' *futa cotovari* 'two reasons,' *mi ami* 'three nets, or three casts of the net,' *iocama* 'to bake something four times in an oven,' *itçu caqe* 'five attacks,' *mu casane* 'six robes, or covers,' *nana catana* 'seven wounds by a sword,' *ia catague* 'eight loads,' *cu cavari*[191] 'nine changes,' *to cusa* 'ten varieties.' Above the number ten this way of counting is not used, instead they say *iro júichi* or *júichi no iro* for 'eleven colors.' The interrogative is *icutçu*. If the thing being questioned is placed after the interrogative the particle *no* is added; e.g., *itçucu no qi zo* [*icutçu* ...] 'how many trees are there?' To such a question the answer is *futatçu* 'two,' *mitçu* 'three,' etc. If the *tçu* is removed from *icutçu*, one may place it in front of the thing being asked about; e.g., *icu tocoro* 'how many places?' *icu toqi* 'how many hours?'; also *fito fanaxi* 'one sermon, or conversation,' *futa sugi* 'two treads,' *io te* 'four hands, as in a fight,' *itçu tçubu* 'five grains,' *mu tocoro* 'six (68 places,' *ia mavari* 'six [eight] circuits,' *cu ninai* 'nine loads, carried in the Japanese fashion on a stick with the load in front,' *to vatari* 'ten crossings.' It is possible to count the same thing in different ways. Thus, *mu tocoro* is also *mutçu no tocoro* and *tocoro mutçu* 'six places.' *Fito ie* means 'one plain thing,' *futa ie* 'doubled, or duplicate,' *mi ie* 'triplicate,' etc. In the same way one may add Chinese numerals to Chinese vocables, or *coie*. Usually in this way of counting a [phonetic] change occurs in either the number or the thing counted. Sometimes this change is in the first part, sometimes in the second, and at other times in both. This is particularly true with the first, second, third, sixth, tenth, and one hundredth numbers. With the items below, if nothing is noted, it is an indication that nothing is changed.

When asking about men one says *icutari?* 'how many men?' The response is made by adding *nin* to the Chinese numeral; e.g., *ichi nin* 'one man,' *ni nin* 'two men,' *iottari* 'four men'; this is because *xinin* means 'dead person.'

When asking about days one says *icca* 'how many days?' The response is *fi fitoi*,[192] because *ichi nichi* means 'one entire solar day,' *futçuca* 'two days,' *micca* 'three days,' *iocca* 'four days,' *itçuca* 'five days,' *muica* 'six days,' *nanuca* 'seven days,' *iŏca* 'eight days,' *coconoca* 'nine days,' *toca*[193] 'ten days,' *fatçuca* 'twenty days.' The remaining days are counted with *coie* numerals.

When counting nights *ia* is added to the *coie* numerals; e.g., *ichi ia* 'one night,' *ni ia* 'two nights,' etc. It is also possible to add *io* which means 'night' in Japanese to the *iomi* numeral; e.g., *icu io* 'how many nights?' *futa io* 'two nights,' *nana io* 'seven nights,' etc.

When enumerating the months of the year *guat* is added to the *coie* numeral, with the exception that the first month is called *xóguat*. The second is *niguat*, the third is *saguat*,[194] the fourth is *xiguat*, the eleventh is *ximotçuqi*, and the twelfth and last is *xi vasu*. When counting months the *tçu* is removed from the *iomi* numeral and the word *tçuqi*, which means 'month,' is added. *Icutçuqi?* means 'how many months.' In response one says *fitotçuqi* 'one month,' up to ten which is *totçuqi*, and from there on one counts with *coie* numerals; e.g., *júichiguat* 'eleven months.' If one wants to ask what month it is, January, February, one says *nanguat*. The first month of the (69 Japanese year is March.

In the enumeration of the years *nen* is placed after the *coie* numeral. In asking how many, *nen* [*nan*] is placed before *nen*; e.g., *nannen* 'how many years?' In response one says *ichinen* 'one year,' *ionen* 'four years,' *sanganen* 'three years,' *sŏ ionen*[195] 'three or four years,' *sŏ xijúnen* 'thirty or forty years,' *fatachi* means 'twenty years of age,' as does *nijŭnen, nijŭ no toxi*, or *toxi niju*. They ask with *icutoxi* or *toxi icutçu* 'how old are you.' They count the age of men and animals such as cattle and horses by adding *sai* to the *coie* numeral; e.g., *issai* 'one,' *nisai* 'two,' *sanzai* 'three.'

In counting turns (*visis*) *do* is added to the *coie* numerals; e.g., *nando* 'how many times,' *ichido* 'once,' *iodo* 'four times,' *godo* 'five times,' *sai san* 'twice or thrice.'

In the enumeration of ships *sô* is placed after the *coie* numeral; e.g., *nanzo* [*nanzô*] 'how many ships,' to which one answers *issô* 'one ship,' *niso* [*nisô*] 'two,' *sanzô* 'three,' *fassô* 'eight,' *jússô* [*jissô*] 'ten.'

*Ichiren* 'one string,' *niren* 'two,' *saren* 'three,' as in figs or pearls.

When enumerating sermons, homilies (*tractatus*), or repetitions of things, *fen* is placed after the numeral; e.g., *ippen* 'one sermon,' *nifen* 'two,' *sanben* 'three,' *ave maria fiacu gojippen* 'one hundred and fifty Hail Mary's.'

In counting gold currency *momme* is placed after the numeral; e.g., *ichi momme* 'one *momme*,' *ni momme* 'two,' *san mome* [*san momme*] 'three.' When a *momme* is divided into tenths it is called an *ippun* [*fun*]. Thus, *ippun* means one tenth part of a *momme*, *nifun* means 'two tenths,' *gofun* means half the basic unit (*media dragma*), *roppun* means 'six tenths of a *momme*.'

When the tenth part of a *momme* is divided again into ten parts it is counted as *ichirin, nirin, sarin, iorin, gorin, rocurin, xichirin, fachirin,* and *curin*. Then comes *ippun*, which is one tenth of a *momme*. *Fiacu me* means 'one hundred *momme*,' *fiacu ichi momme* 'one hundred and one,' *icquan me* means 'one thousand *momme*,' *jicquanme* means 'ten thousand.' There are other coins of silver which are counted by placing *mai* or *mon* after the numeral; e.g., *ichi mon* means one of that unit, *ni mon* is 'two,' *San mai* is three hundred *mon*. They no longer produce a coin which is one half of the gold coin, but one thousand of these coins make *icquan*, while *jicquan* is 'ten (70 thousand *quan*.'[196]

*Core va ica fodo ni suru* 'how much is this worth?' or *ica fodo ni uru* 'at what price will you sell this?' *Ni momme suru* 'I consider it worth two *momme*,' or *ni momme ni iasui* 'I can sell this for more than two *momme*, or at two *momme* this is cheap.'

The enumeration of liquid measurements is done by placing the particle *xô* in front of the liquid quantity; e.g., *ixxo* [*ixxô*] 'one *xô*,' *nixo* [*nixô*] 'two,' *sango* [*sanjô*] 'three.' Ten *xô* are *itto* which is the particle *to* placed after the numeral; *nito* means 'twenty *xô*,' *sando* 'thirty.' For one tenth of a *xô* one places the particle *go* after the numeral; e.g., *Ichigo* 'one *go*,' *nigo* 'two,' *sango* 'three,' *ixxô gogo* 'one and one half *xô*.' *Fatto* is eighty *xô*. One hundred *xô* make *ichi cocu*. By placing the *cocu* after numerals one obtains *ni cocu* 'two hundred *xô*,' *sangocu* 'three hundred,' *jiccocu* 'one thousand,' *xencocu* 'ten thousand,' *ichi mangocu* 'one hundred thousand.'

The enumeration of the measurements of human height is achieved by placing *fito* [*firo*] after the *iomi* numerals; e.g., *fito firo* 'one *firo*,' *futa firo* 'two,' *jippiro* 'ten.' The measurement of a span (*palmus*) is made by adding *xacu* to the *coie* numerals; e.g., *ixxacu* 'one span, or three spans by the Spanish measuring system,'[197] *sanjaku* 'three.' *Goxacu* is the same as *fito firo* which is a measurement we have referred to before. Six *xacu* make up a measurement called *icqen* 'one *qen*,' *nicqen* [*niqen*] 'two,' *jicqen* 'ten,' and *sanguen* 'three.' From sixty of these measurements one makes a measurement called *icchó*, that is 'one mountain path,' *nicchŏ* [*nichŏ*] 'two,' *jichiŏ [jicchŏ]* 'ten,' *sangiŏ* 'three.' From sixty-three [thirty-six] *chô*, as measured in the northern part of Japan, one obtains *ichiri* which is one league or one miliar. One enumerates by adding *ri* to the *coie* numerals; e.g., *niri* 'two,' *sanri* 'three,' *gori* 'five,' *júri* 'ten'; *iori* is 'four,' because *xiri* means anus.[198] *Fan michi* means 'a half of a league.' They say; *ioco fan miqi tate ichiri* [... *michi* ...] 'a half a *ri* wide and one *ri* long,' *faba icqen* 'the width is one *qen*,' *iofŏ futa firo* 'two *hiro* on all sides.'

The cardinal numbers first, second, etc. are made by adding *ban* to the *coie* numerals; e.g., *ichi ban* 'first,' *ni ban* 'second.' To these are also added *me*, as said before; e.g., *xi ban me* 'fourth.' One may also make the cardinal numbers by placing *dai* in front of the *coie* (71 numerals; e.g., *daiichi* 'first,' *daini* 'second,' etc.

The enumeration of multiples is done by adding *bai* to the numbers; e.g., *ichibai* 'double,' *nibai* 'triple,' *sanbai* 'quadruple,'[199] *fiacu zobai* 'one hundred fold.'

The enumeration of the parts from the whole is done by placing *buichi* after the numeral; e.g., *ni buichi* 'one from two parts,' *san buichi* 'one from three parts.'

To indicate one tenth *vari* is placed after the numeral; e.g., *ichi vari* 'one from ten parts,' *xi vari gobu* 'four and one half from ten parts.' *Jú buichi* is the same as *ichi vari*.

The enumeration of oars, muskets, and long things made of wood is done by placing *chó* after the numerals; e.g., *icchó* 'one oar,' *nichó* 'two,' *sangiŏ* 'three,' *jichó* [*jicchó*] 'ten.'

The enumeration of fish and fire wood is done by placing *con* after the numerals;[200] e.g., *iccon*, 'one fish,' *sangon* 'three,' *jiccon* 'ten,' *fiaccon* 'one hundred,' *fiacu gojŭ sangon* 'one hundred and fifty-three.' This is the amount Saint Peter caught, and even though he caught that number the net did not tear.

The enumeration of leaves of paper and sheets of gold, etc. is done by placing *mai* after the numeral; e.g., *ichimai* 'one leaf,' *cami gomai* 'five leaves of paper.'

The enumeration of the stories of a house is done by placing *cai* after the numeral; e.g., *nicai* 'the first floor,' *sangai* 'the second,' *xigai* 'the third,' *gocai* 'the fourth,' when counted as in a house in Madrid.

The enumeration of utensils and cups for drinking is done by placing *fai* after the numeral; e.g., *ippai* 'one drink, or one draught,' *nifai* 'two,' *sanbai* 'three,' *jippai* 'ten.'

The enumeration of rolls of silk or the like is done by placing *tan* after the numeral; e.g., *ittan* 'one roll,' *nitan* 'two,' *sandan* 'three,' *jittan* 'ten.' *Xichitan bune* is a ship with a sail seven *tan* wide.

This is also said by adding *mai* to the numeral; e.g., *gomai* 'five,' as in *gomai bune* 'a ship having a sail five *mai* wide.'

The enumeration of four-footed animals is done by placing *fiqi* after the numeral; e.g., *ippiqi* 'one animal,' *nifiqi* 'two,' *sanbiqi* 'three,' *roppiqi* 'six,' *jippiqi* 'ten,' *fiappiqi* 'one hundred,' *xenbiqi* 'one thousand.'

The enumeration of images, pictures, and medicines is done (72 by placing *fucu* after the numeral; e.g., *ippucu* 'one item,' *nifucu* 'two,' *sanbucu* 'three,' *roppucu* 'six,' *jippucu* 'ten.' Needles are also counted this way.

The enumeration of pounds (*libra*) is done by placing *qin* after the numeral; e.g., *icqin* 'one pound,' *niqin* 'two,' *sanguin* 'three,' *rocqin* 'six,' *jicqin* 'ten,' *fiacqin* 'one hundred,' *xenqin* 'one thousand.'

The enumeration of masses and congregations of men is done by placing *za* after the numeral; e.g., *ichiza* 'one congregation,' *niza* 'two,' *sanza* 'three,' *jŭza*, or better *toza* 'ten.'

The enumeration of sacks of rice, wheat, and the like, is done by placing *fiô* after the numeral; e.g., *ippiô* 'one sack,' *nifiô* 'two,' *sanbiô* 'three,' *xifio* [*xifiô*] 'four,' *roppio* [*roppiô*] 'six,' *jippio* [*jippiô*] 'ten,' *fiiappio* [*fiappiô*] 'one hundred,' *xembiô* [*xenbiô*] 'one thousand.'

The enumeration of pieces of wood, reeds, and needles is done by placing *fon* after the numeral; e.g., *ippon* 'one item,' *nifon* 'two,' *sanbon* 'three,' *roppon* 'six,' *jippon* 'ten,' *fiappon* 'one hundred,' *xenbon* 'one thousand.'

The enumeration of bundles (*fasciculus*) is done by placing *va* after the numeral; e.g., *ichiva* 'one bundle,' *niva* 'two,' *sanba* 'three,' *jippa* 'ten,' *júichiva* 'eleven,' *ni jippa* 'twenty.'

The enumeration of burdens or the packs that horses carry is done by placing *só* after the numeral; e.g., *issó* 'one burden,' *nisŏ* 'two,' *sanzó* 'three,' *jissŏ* 'ten.' In the same way one counts those furnishings called *biŏbu*; two or a pair from a set is called *issó*, etc.

The enumeration of that which in the vernacular is called a quire of paper (*mano de papel*) is done by placing *giô* after the numeral; e.g., *ichigio* [*ichigiô*] 'one quire,' *nigio* [*nigiô*] 'two,' *sangiô* 'three,' so on to ten. Units of ten are counted by adding *socu* to the numeral; e.g., *issocu* 'ten quires, or what in the vernacular is called a half ream (*media resma*),' *nisocu* 'twenty, or an entire ream.' With this particle *socu* added to numerals one also counts pairs of shoes; e.g., *issocu* 'a pair of shoes.'

The enumeration of substance (*substantia*) is done by placing *tai* after the numeral; e.g., *ittai* 'one substance,' *nitai* 'two,' *sandai* 'three.' *Deus no von tocoro va goittai de gozaru* 'God as God is of one substance and one essence.'

The enumeration of the divisions in a writing (*capitulum*) is done by placing *cagiô* after the numeral; e.g., *iccagiô* 'one chapter,' (73 *nicagio* [*nicagiô*] 'two,' *sangagio* [*sangagiô*] 'three,' *roccagio* [*roccagiô*] 'six,' *fiaccagio* [*fiaccagiô*] 'one hundred.'

The enumeration of drops is done by placing *teqi* after the numeral; e.g., *itteqi* 'one drop,' *jitteqi* 'ten.' The same meaning is obtained by adding *xizzucu* to the *iomi* numeral; e.g., *fito xizzucu* 'one drop,' etc. In this case the *tçu* must be removed from the numeral.

The enumeration of the pairs of small sticks (*paxillus*) with which they eat is done by placing *tçui* after the numeral; e.g., *itçui* [*ittçui*] 'one pair,' *jittçui* 'ten.'

The enumeration of bundles is done by placing *ca* after the numeral; e.g., *icca* 'one bundle,' *nica* 'two,' *sanga* 'three.'

The enumeration of books is done by placing *quan* after the numeral; e.g., *icquan* 'one book,' *niquan* 'two,' *sanguan* 'three,' *roquan* [*rocquan*] 'six,' *jiquan* [*jicquan*] 'ten.'

With the interrogative *nan*, when it is placed before one of these nouns, it changes it in the same way as does the number three; e.g., *ano mmadomo va nanbiki zo?* 'how many horses are there?'

The enumeration of kingdoms (*regnum*) is done by placing *cacocu* after the numeral; e.g., *iccacocu* 'one kingdom,' *nicacocu* 'two,' *sangacocu* 'three,' *jiccacocu* 'ten.' Kingdoms are divided into provinces or districts called *gun*, and this word also is placed after the numeral; e.g., *ichigun* 'one province,' *nigun* 'two,' *sangun* 'three,' etc.

Sermons and exhortations are enumerated by placing *dan* after the numeral; *ichidan* 'one sermon, or assembly.' Words are enumerated by placing *gon* or *guen* after the numeral; e.g., *ichigon* 'one word,' *sanguen* 'three words.'

Placing the particle *zzutçu* after either *coie* or *iomi* numerals gives the meaning of 'each'; e.g., *ichinin ni uxi sanbiki zzutçu vo toraxeta* 'he let the men have three oxen each,' *ichinin zzutçu saqe sanbai zzutçu vo nomareta* 'each man drank three sake each.'

In speaking of two or three things separately, they join the two numbers; e.g., *xigonin* 'four or five men,' from which others may be copied.

The honorific particles are four; *vo, von, go*, and *mi*.[201] The first two are joined to *iomi* vocables. The last two are joined to *coie*, or Chinese vocables. The last is the most honorific and is used when speaking of things divine; e.g., *midexi tachi* 'disciples of Christ the Lord,' *goichinin vocoite cudasarei* 'please send one from among the Lords.'

The words which follow have honorific particles that have (74 been added by the speaker. However, the honor is shown to the person addressed or to those related to him; e.g., *go focô* [*go fôcô*] 'a duty,' *von furu mai* 'a banquet,' *von cotoba* 'a word, or a sermon,' *von mono gatari* 'a conversation,' *von natçucaxij* or *von nocori vovoi* which mean the same as what the Portuguese call *saudades* (nostalgia) and the Spanish call *carino* (affection), *von tori avaxe* 'intercession,' *von mi mai* 'a visit,' *von cha* 'that which one drinks when they invite you,' *go dancó* 'a consultation or congregation for the purpose of obtaining advice,' *von rei* 'an act of gratitude,' *von busata* 'a lapse of good manners,' *vo motenaxi* 'to treat well and elegantly,' *go chiso* [*go chisô*] 'esteem,' *go iqen* 'an opinion,' e.g., *fabacari nagara go iqen vo mǒxitai* 'forgive me but I would like to give you some advice,' etc.

# Some Rules on the Conjugation of the Verb in the Written Language

If the final *u* is removed from the negative present it becomes an affirmative verb; e.g., *oracio vo tçutomen toqi va* 'when I say my prayers,' *xosa no tçutomen tame ni va* 'in order to execute the work,' *michibiqi tamavan to voboximexi* 'thinking of leading forth.'[202]

For the affirmative future *beqi* is added to the affirmative form with the *ru* removed; for the future negative *becarazu* is added to the affirmative form; e.g., *mŏsu beqi* 'you will speak,' *mósu becarazu* 'you will not speak.' When the sentence ends in the future, *beqi* is changed to *bexi*.

The infinitive for the future is formed by adding *coto* to the future tense; e.g., *iomu beqi coto*. The subjunctive is formed by adding *qereba* to the root of the verb; e.g., *sugure qereba*.

The gerund in *Do* is formed by adding *te* to the root of the verb; e.g., *qiqi tamaite*.

The substantive verb in the written language is *nari,u* or *qeri,u*. If it comes at the end of the sentence it takes the root form;[203] e.g., *sadame naqi io no ixei nari* 'it is the dignity of a world without stability.'

The preterit is formed by adding *ari,u* [*tari,u*] to the root; e.g., *suguretaru*. If the form comes at the end of a sentence *ari,u* (75 [*tari,u*] is retained in the root form; e.g., *suguretari*.

The pluperfect is formed by placing *nari* after the present tense; e.g., *ague tamŏ nari* 'they had shown respect.'

Even though there are other rules for the written language, if the reader knows Japanese well enough to read books, he will be able to progress in the language without difficulty.

***PRAISE BE TO GOD***